Psychology in Coaching Practice

Coaching Psychology for Professional Practice

Series editor: Dr Manfusa Shams, FHEA, AFBPsS, C.Psychol, CSci

Psychology in Coaching Practice

A Guide for Professionals

Manfusa Shams

Open University Press

Open University Press
McGraw Hill
Unit 4,
Foundation Park
Roxborough Way
Maidenhead
SL6 3UD

email: emea_uk_ireland@mheducation.com
world wide web: www.openup.co.uk

First edition published 2022

A catalogue record of this book is available from the British Library

ISBN-13: 978-0-3352-5118-6
ISBN-10: 0335251188
eISBN: 978-0-3352-5119-3

Library of Congress Cataloging-in-Publication Data
CIP data applied for

Typeset by Transforma Pvt. Ltd., Chennai, India

Praise page

This book is very timely with its key focus on coaching practice underpinned by coaching psychology. Whether you're an experienced practitioner, or a coach or coaching psychologist in training, this book will be a valuable resource. With its focus on professional and ethical practice it successfully integrates the power of client characteristics, pluralistic insights and the impact of our ever-changing society on coaching and coaching outcomes.

Mary Watts, Emeritus Professor of Psychology, City University of London

Psychology in Coaching Practice: A Guide for Professionals ***offers a well-considered selection of chapters that reflect the experience as well as the knowledge of the authors and editors. The book aims to cultivate understanding of coaching psychology as a professional practice and to enhance the knowledge and skills of practitioners and is appropriate for a broad range of professionals in the field. Written with a pragmatic orientation, the chapters explore multiple aspects of coaching psychology including theory, application and ethics and provide a practitioner model as a framework for professional engagement. The book also includes chapters on topics rarely addressed elsewhere, including the impact of client personality on coaching outcomes and a pluralistic perspective on coaching psychology practice. The chapter exploring the impact of proliferating technologies is highly relevant to practice.***

Francine Campone, EdD, MCC, Accredited Coaching Supervisor Editor, International Coaching Psychology Review

This book has been written by experts in the coaching and coaching psychology field. As it focuses on the professional development of practitioners, it will be of great interest to both trainees and experienced practitioners. Professionals working in areas allied to coaching may also find it of interest.

Professor Stephen Palmer PhD, Centre for Coaching, London

Manfusa Shams' book provides fresh insights to the specialist area of coaching psychology practice, providing readers with practical insights into working with individuals, the team and wider social system to help each move forward towards personal and business success. The focus on psychology in practice in this book is an important development to advance this discipline.

Professor Jonathan Passmore, SVP CoachHub and Professor, Henley Business School, England

For myself (Manfusa)

Contents

Introducing the Coaching Psychology for Professional Practice series: Series editor's foreword

Coaching psychology is a relatively new discipline. Coaching involves the application of relevant psychological principles, theories and concepts, hence it is essential to develop a discipline-based approach to deliver psychological input in coaching. This has resulted in the formal recognition of coaching psychology as an applied scientific discipline, with the aim of supporting growth and development for the effective functioning of individuals as a result of coaching.

The Coaching Psychology for Professional Practice series aims to offer a unique opportunity for psychologists and practitioners to learn, share and contribute to critical coaching practice issues using appropriate psychological knowledge. The remit of the series is not limited to the psychology discipline, but extends to a wide range of disciplines, services and service users (human development, education, health, public services, occupation and business, global economy, international relations). The goal of this series is thus far-reaching: to inform, educate and popularize the positive outcomes of the application of coaching psychology to change, maintain and improve human potential. The content of each book in the series will be underpinned by relevant theories and models, with a focus on 'application and practice'. They will be written by experts and specialists in coaching psychology and coaching practice, using relevant knowledge and understanding, research evidence, case studies, professional development and practice activities.

The main objectives of this series are:

- To consolidate ideas to develop a firm applied knowledge base in coaching psychology.
- To bridge the gap between theory and practice in coaching psychology.
- To develop, promote and popularize the benefits of coaching practice to optimize human potential, and growth in effective human functioning.
- To take a lead in delivering practice-related critical issues in coaching psychology.
- To provide a platform to share good practice in coaching, using a critical and reflective practitioner's approach.
- To disseminate knowledge about coaching psychology practice to a wide range of readers across the globe.

Psychology in Coaching Practice is the first book in this series. The book aims to highlight the psychological basis of coaching practice, and the theoretical grounding of coaching psychology practice. The focus is on the influence of psychology in coaching psychology knowledge construction and developing effective coaching psychology practice.

Dr Manfusa Shams
Series editor: Coaching Psychology for Professional Practice

Preface

The celebration of human potential to advance behavioural development and to change for personal growth is the main attraction in the study of coaching psychology. The delivery of specialist knowledge in coaching psychology through coaching practice is reaffirming the unique position of coaching psychology to support the progress of individuals and groups in an increasingly competitive and hostile environment. Coaching psychology thus opens up a new era for understanding human behaviour using a pragmatic and progressive approach.

The primary developmental task for coaching psychology is to inform and educate all in society about the immense value of coaching psychology practice. This needs to be accomplished using effective delivery of practice, research, educational programmes and publications which have policy implications on making changes in the key developmental areas, such as health and education. A strong theoretical grounding in coaching psychology is required to provide the theory-driven coaching practice, and to offer developmental opportunity in coaching psychology as it progresses to support untying complex knots in biopsychosocial aspects of human potential. The fundamental question of what is coaching psychology practice can be answered using evidence-based discussion on the influence of psychology knowledge in coaching practice. The very presence of psychology in coaching practice is the major feature of this book. *Psychology in Coaching Practice* is the first book in this series, Coaching Psychology for Professional Practice.

The focus of this book is to deliver practice-based knowledge and ethical guidance to inform professional coaching practice, and to advance coaching practice using relevant psychological paradigms. The main aim is to present the psychological basis of coaching practice using a practitioner's perspective, and to highlight the influence of psychology knowledge in developing and delivering effective coaching practice.

The book is expected to provide a valuable and useful resource for practitioners, academics, researchers, businesses, organizations and anyone interested in applying coaching psychology to their respective areas. It will serve as a professional guide to navigate through human functioning to support individuals to reach their optimum performance level, and to increase their developmental lifeline. Each chapter is focused on providing learning impetus and a shared knowledge base to promote the application of coaching psychology. The distinctive feature of this book is the practical application of knowledge in relation to coaching psychology, an ethical approach in coaching practice, the theoretical basis of coaching psychology practice, and practice-related, evidence-based critical reflective discussions.

Psychology in Coaching Practice offers a rich collection of resources for coaching psychologists and practitioners to learn and share, and to develop critical reflective skills to apply to their own practice.

The plan for the book is drawn from my long and extensive academic, research, supervision, mentoring, publications and other professional work as a psychologist, author and editor, mentor and group facilitator to develop coaching psychology as a distinctive practice-based discipline. Over the years, I have found a growing interest in articulating the key issues in coaching psychology to benefit practitioners, and to deliver relevant theory-driven and practice-related, evidence-based knowledge to improve the application of coaching psychology. This interest was reinforced by my continuous engagement with the special group in coaching psychology, reviews and editorial work for *The Coaching Psychologist* and *International Coaching Psychology Review* journals, delivering my professional workshops, and work for the psychological testing centre of the British Psychological Society. My long and rich academic experience has enabled me to identify the need to document and publish knowledge and practice-related critical issues systematically for educational and research purposes along with improving coaching psychology practice. Furthermore, the valuable support from McGraw-Hill and Open International Publishing Ltd to launch a new 'Coaching Psychology for Professional Practice' series, for which I was offered the series editor role, has enabled me to plan, develop and deliver this book.

Theoretical models and thoughtful analysis for practice, with real-life case studies, are valuable to a wide range of readers. Each chapter is designed to highlight the value of psychology in professional coaching practice using appropriate case studies from coaching practice.

All the chapters in this book present illuminating and progressive discussions on the current position of coaching psychology practice, and offer thoughtful, forward-looking theoretical analysis and models, ethical codes and issues in coaching practice, along with practitioners' valuable experience in selected critical issues in practice. The main theme running through the chapters is 'psychology in coaching practice', and the major contribution of psychological knowledge to planning, developing and executing theory-driven coaching practice. Critical discussions on current knowledge and practice of coaching psychology in the digital world, and local and global coaching practices, are an added attraction of this book.

The structure of the book is based on academic rigour in articulating fundamental coaching psychology issues in selected areas. The primary focus is to inform and benefit aspiring practitioners with rich evidence-based critical discussions to facilitate the practitioners' journey to achieve competency and professional accountability, and to appreciate the benefits of applying psychological knowledge to develop and maintain good ethical practice in coaching.

Writing a book requires tireless effort and high commitment to complete a long writing journey. However, with contributions from a few leading coaching practitioners, it was a pleasant and rewarding experience. I was pleased to engage myself with writing this book at a challenging time when we have had to continuously negotiate with the rapidly changing, unpredictable environment. This was a difficult time, during the Covid-19 pandemic, with uncertain and unexpected natural calamities looming over us, making our existence a challenge. Nonetheless, these challenges and risks provide impetus to generate innovative ideas, bringing critical thoughtful understanding of advancing coaching psychology practice to a new level of development and progress.

My personal learning from writing this book extends beyond the delivery of relevant knowledge to develop excellent partnerships with all my authors and publishing team. Their encouragement, timely, engaging and supportive responses, and availabilities have helped me to complete the book within the set deadline. I am grateful to all my authors for their scholarly presence in their chapters, and their valuable time, energy and cooperation.

I have managed to articulate my ideas of the need for a strong theoretical basis for coaching psychology practice in my proposed new 'selective realism model' (Chapter 4). It was a rewarding experience to be able to deliver the much-needed 'psychology in coaching practice' book, and in opening up new areas of research and practice. The fundamental issue of putting theory into practice is addressed in this book, which will ensure best practice in coaching psychology.

As a primer of the Coaching Psychology for Professional Practice series, this book is expected to be invaluable in its contribution to current coaching psychology knowledge and practice.

Manfusa Shams, 2022, England

Acknowledgements

I am very grateful to Laura Pacey, head of publishing, for her encouragement, support and interest in launching this new series of Coaching Psychology for Professional Practice. My special thanks to Eleanor Christie and Zoe Osman for their constant and timely support, valuable guidance and advice. My gratitude to all my authors – Dave Tee, Bruce Grimley, Tony Fusco, Toni Clarkson, Andrea Giraldez-Hayes and Wendy-Ann Smith – for their invaluable time, commitment, interests and scholarly contributions. Finally, I am grateful to Professor Mary Watts, Professor Jonathan Passmore, Professor Stephen Palmer and Dr Francine Campone for their valuable supportive endorsements.

About the author and contributors

Author and series editor: Manfusa Shams

Manfusa Shams is a Chartered Psychologist, Series Editor *for Coaching Psychology for Professional Practice book series* (McGraw Hill Open University Press), Consulting editor of *The Coaching Psychologist* and an editorial board member of the *International Coaching Psychology Review* (British Psychological Society). She has published numerous books and journal articles. A few major publications are books, *Development in work and organisational psychology: Implications for international business* (Emerald), *Coaching in the family-owned business and Supporting the family business: A coaching practitioner's handbook* (Routledge). Manfusa is an experienced author, editor, supervisor, reviewer, coach, mentor and group facilitator. She is a Fellow of the Higher Education Academy, UK, and a member of the Division of Coaching Psychology (British Psychological Society). She holds academic position at the Open University and Reading University.

Contributors

Toni Clarkson

Toni Clarkson is a coaching psychologist with over 20 years' experience working at leadership level. Toni has worked extensively in the public, private and not-for-profit sectors with a wide range of managers, leaders and teams, ranging from the NHS, government, private sector, MOD, military, and scientific research establishments as well as mental health/registered care organizations. Her background and experience encompass a range of areas within OD but her main interest and expertise lie in coaching and leadership.

In addition to working with her own coaching clients, Toni also develops, qualifies and supervises coaches, with a focus on enabling skilled and passionate coaches. Having auditioned many theoretical approaches and modalities over the years, Toni has found her psychological and praxis home in relational gestalt.

Tony Fusco

Tony Fusco is a professional coaching psychologist, leadership coach and facilitator with 20 years' experience coaching managers and leaders in both the public and private sectors. He is chartered by the British Psychological Society and registered and accredited by the International Society for Coaching Psychology. For his doctorate in coaching psychology he developed the first evidence-based approach to authentic leadership development (ALD). The research and development of this group coaching approach to ALD has been peer-reviewed and published in various coaching journals and a 2018 Routledge book entitled *An Evidence-Based Approach to Authentic Leadership Development.* He works as a leadership development tutor across many sectors and organizations ranging from central government, health care, the police and the NHS to engineering, manufacturing and the nuclear, oil and gas sectors.

Andrea Giraldez-Hayes

Andrea Giraldez-Hayes is a chartered psychologist. She is Director of the Well-being and Psychological Services Centre and the MSc in Applied Positive Psychology and Coaching Psychology at the University of East London. She is a well-being coach with special interest in the application of arts and creativity in coaching and positive psychology. Andrea is an associate editor of *Coaching: An International Journal of Theory, Research and Practice* (Taylor & Francis), *International Coaching Psychology Review* (British Psychological Society), *International Journal of Coaching Psychology* (NWS) and the *Journal of Positive School Psychology.* She is also a member of the Division of Coaching Psychology's committee (British Psychological Society). Andrea has published more than 50 books and papers and is a renowned international public speaker at conferences in the UK, Europe and Latin America.

Bruce Grimley

Bruce Grimley is a Chartered Occupational Psychologist registered with the Health and Care Professions Council (HCPC). He is the author of two books and numerous chapters and papers on the topic of coaching psychology. Bruce is also a senior practitioner of psychotherapy on the Register of Psychologists Specialising in Psychotherapy. He was a director of the Neuro-Linguistic Psychotherapy and Counselling Association, which is an organizational member of the UK Council for Psychotherapy (UKCP), for over three years (2017–20). Bruce has been Managing Director of Achieving Lives Ltd, a thriving psychology business, for 25 years.

Wendy-Ann Smith

Wendy-Ann is a coach, psychologist and director of Eclorev, a coaching, consulting boutique. She enjoys collaborating in consulting projects. Wendy-Ann is a co-founder of the Coaching Ethics Forum (CEF), where she led and coordinated an international team to produce the first international conference dedicated to ethics in coaching. She has edited two volumes: Positive Psychology Coaching in the Workplace (Springer) and The Ethical Coaches' Handbook: A Guide to Developing Ethical Maturity in Practice (Routledge). Wendy-Ann regularly coaches a small number of one-to-one clients. She designs and delivers lectures, trainings and workshops in a variety of international settings. She is interested in supporting the development of coaches with coaching psychology, positive psychology, and increasing ethical practice.

David Tee

David Tee is the Global Director of Science at CoachHub. In addition, he is a Visiting Fellow at the University of South Wales and Visiting Lecturer at the University of Worcester. He is the editor of research publication *The Coaching Psychologist*, and co-editor of two books, *Coaching Researched* (2020) and *Coaching Practised* (2022) (both John Wiley & Sons).

Introduction

Manfusa Shams

Coaching psychology is an emerging practice-based discipline. The developmental journey, along with highlights of both the theoretical and the practical side of this discipline, is presented in this book. The aim is to introduce, inform and enlighten readers about coaching psychology as a valuable professional practice, and to encourage, accept, acknowledge and embrace coaching psychology as a valuable scientific discipline.

The series is focused on coaching psychology practitioners, hence it is important to provide an opening text in which relevant introductory issues for practice are critically discussed, analysed and evaluated, followed by a set of practice-related topics to exemplify the application of coaching psychology.

This first book in the series, *Psychology in Coaching Practice*, presents practice-based knowledge and guidance to inform professional coaching practice, and to advance coaching practice using relevant psychological theories and models. It is predominantly designed to support coaching practice using relevant schools of thought, psychological models, theories, case studies and practitioners' reflective analyses. The discussions in all chapters are guided by coaching psychology principles, with a focus on practical applications to coaching practice.

Aims

The main aim is to present the theoretical basis of coaching psychology, and theory-driven coaching psychology practice.

The book also aims to provide authoritative knowledge about good ethical practice and the professional standing of coaching psychology.

This book is expected to be useful to various fields of practice, e.g. education, health, public services, occupational and business, global economy and human resources.

Each chapter is written to demonstrate the value of psychological knowledge in a selected area of professional coaching practice. This is achieved through an overview of the historical development of coaching psychology, critical discussions on existing practice, thoughtful development of theoretical models and the practitioner's reflective, in-depth understanding of good ethical practice in coaching psychology.

Major features

The distinctive feature is the practical application of knowledge in relation to coaching psychology, and practice-related evidence-based critical reflective discussion.

The highlight of this book is evidence-based discussion and practitioners' reflective experiential accounts of using the theoretical basis of coaching psychology. The need for strong theoretical groundwork for coaching psychology is argued, for the development and recognition of this scientific discipline. The introduction of two new theoretical models to support a shift in psychology paradigm for understanding human behaviour using a coaching lens, and to value the implication of coaching practice for improving holistic performance are striking features of this book.

The book is written for practitioners by practitioners to assert the need for a theoretical basis to coaching psychology practice, and to put relevant psychological theories into coaching practice to promote best ethical practice in coaching psychology.

The book has two parts. Part I is focused on the 'practice' to present relevant schools of thought, psychological models, research evidence and critical issues in coaching practice. The 'application' section in Part II offers selected intellectual contributions from leading practitioners to present the application of psychological theory to coaching practice, and evidence-based discussions on best practice in coaching psychology.

Each chapter is underpinned by relevant theories, models and research evidence, with a focus on 'application and practice', and written by experts and specialists in coaching psychology. The discussion in all chapters is expected to generate ideas and interest to apply psychological knowledge to coaching practice systematically, with an acknowledgement of powerful psychological input in effective coaching practice.

The book provides valuable insights into the theoretical basis of coaching psychology practice, and the emerging value of coaching psychology to develop and advance individuals. Critical discussions, thoughtful analyses and a deep knowledge base, with relevant practice-based case studies, address the need for theorizing coaching psychology, and place coaching psychology firmly in the psychology discipline domain. The application of theory into practice and theory-driven coaching tools and techniques will be useful to develop and improve practice, with a strong focus on ethics in coaching psychology practice. The book is an essential companion to coaching psychology practice, and a landmark starting point for psychology in coaching practice.

Part I

Practice

Introduction

The main aim of Part I is to provide evidence-based discussion on the influence of psychology in coaching practice, and show how coaching psychology knowledge is constructed and informed by different psychological schools of thoughts. The most salient feature of this part is introducing a new conceptual coaching psychology model for practice (Chapter 4).

The discussion in each chapter is supported by relevant psychological concepts and theories, research evidence and ethical issues to affirm the position of coaching psychology as a distinctive branch of psychology.

Chapter 1 introduces coaching psychology as a distinctive area of psychology, and highlights the influence of psychological knowledge, principles, theories and models in coaching practice. The chapter opens up the discussion on the influence of psychology in coaching practice, highlighting the essential features of coaching psychology practice, and asserting that coaching psychology is a specialist branch of psychology. The discussion separates the popular usage of 'coaching' from 'coaching psychology', to strengthen the ground of coaching psychology as a distinctive area of psychology. The chapter concludes that the search for the answer to the critical question, 'where is psychology in coaching?' can lead to a paradigm shift in understanding an individual's development, and this is presented in Chapter 4. Chapter 2 continues the discussion in coaching psychology knowledge construction using a few specific schools of thought, such as humanistic psychology and positive psychology. The ethical and professional issues in relation to coaching psychology practice are presented in Chapter 3. This chapter sets out the requirement to obtain accreditation from the relevant professional body to practise coaching psychology, which is expected to provide ethical and professional regulations in conjunction with a set of standard good practice in coaching psychology. Coaching psychology requires a solid theoretical foundation specific to this discipline. In Chapter 4, we propose a new theoretical paradigm to present a fully functional individual in the developmental timeline to respond to appropriate coaching interventions using reconstructed live experiences, and understanding of self in the light of new experiences. The proposed model is called 'selective realism' to trace multiple changes during and after the coaching interventions. The expected changes affect neurological, cognitive and behavioural functions in an individual.

Psychology in coaching practice

Manfusa Shams

Summary

This first chapter begins the discussion on the influence of psychology in coaching practice. It presents the arguments in favour of coaching psychology as a distinctive scientific discipline, regulated by psychological principles, levels of analysis, and driven by psychological knowledge. The chapter concludes that coaching practice is informed by psychological knowledge, and coaching psychology is an important applied science for understanding human development using a coaching perspective.

Keywords: psychology in coaching, coaching psychology, coaching practice, psychological principles, coaching practitioners.

Introduction

Coaching psychology is steadily developing as an emerging practice-based discipline. This new discipline is taking a valuable position within the psychology discipline and it has a cascade effect. Coaching practice cascades down different knowledge bases in psychology, such as work and organizational psychology, health and educational psychology. This confirms that coaching psychology is predominantly a psychological discipline with multitudes of variant practices that are informed by different sub-disciplines of psychology. It is important to identify the psychological basis of coaching practice to assert that coaching practice is guided by psychological knowledge and principles.

Aims

This chapter aims to discuss how coaching psychology is built on psychological principles and levels of analysis. Using relevant research evidence, it presents persuasive arguments in favour of coaching psychology as a distinctive branch of psychology.

Coaching psychology is a practice-based scientific discipline

Coaching is the process of supporting individuals to develop and grow to their full potential without any clinical or therapeutic interventions. The meeting point of psychology and coaching is the individual, and this brings the justified application of psychological knowledge, principles, theories and models to deliver coaching to individuals and groups.

Psychology has the competitive advantage to support human excellence in all areas, including the potential for innovation and creativity. All natural and social sciences are required to apply psychological knowledge, either directly or indirectly, when these disciplines are exploring, investigating, and discussing individuals' and groups' functioning in various contexts. For example, the national economy is reliant on business functions of organizations, trade and commerce, innovative and creative business development, etc. This is accomplished using the governance, management and economic behaviour of individuals and groups in those organizations. The knowledge required in this context can be served by occupational and organizational psychology, work and business psychology, and social psychology. Similarly, an innovation in a natural science discipline such as medicine is dedicated to improving patients' physical health conditions. However, the treatment success depends on the patient's adherence to treatment, and their recovery/improvement both physically and psychologically. The existing multi-agency services in the health sector in most developed countries include psychology services in the delivery of effective health and social care. Unlike any other discipline, psychology thus has the greatest competitive advantage because psychology studies individuals and group behaviour, and all disciplines consider human behaviour at various stages of their disciplinary interventions.

Coaching psychology is delivering the most appropriate psychologically grounded practical applications. It is a practice-based scientific discipline with a primary focus on supporting individuals to achieve their optimum level of functioning. Hence development and enhancement are the two major features of coaching psychology. Psychological knowledge must be used appropriately in coaching practice to facilitate and enhance human performance – for example, psychological knowledge and understanding of leadership behaviour and group functions are essential to deliver team coaching (Shams 2022). Coaching practice cannot be validated without the application of psychological principles. Psychology is the essence of coaching practice, and this is confirmed through coaching psychology research and practice.

The following sections will discuss, explore and evaluate each major psychological principle in relation to coaching practice.

Psychology principles and goals

Psychology is a leading scientific discipline with practical applications in everyday life. This evidence-based discipline informs us about all issues affecting our professional lives, family relationships and emotional well-being (American Psychological Association 2021).

The major principles of general psychology:

- Principle 1: Behaviour is observable
- Principle 2: Behaviour can be measured
- Principle 3: Behaviour can be investigated/explored
- Principle 4: Behaviour can be changed/modified
- Principle 5: Behavioural outcomes can be repeated and replicated

Psychology strives to apply these principles to achieve the following five key goals:

- Goal 1: To describe individuals' and groups' behaviour
- Goal 2: To understand the causes of behaviour
- Goal 3: To predict how people and other species will behave in different environmental conditions
- Goal 4: To apply scientific techniques to influence behaviour
- Goal 5: To advance human behaviour using psychological knowledge (Holt et al. 2019).

The primary goal of coaching psychology is to facilitate the development of individuals and groups, which is influenced by psychological and environmental factors. Hence, the focus is on individuals and groups exclusively (Goal 1). Using relevant psychological theory and conceptual understanding, coaching psychology offers explanations for the changes in behaviour as a result of coaching interventions (Goal 2). It is possible to predict the changes in behaviour through coaching intervention (Goal 3). Coaching psychology is about applying relevant tools and techniques to ensure behavioural changes and progression in the desired behaviour (Goal 4). Coaching psychology thus applies psychological principles to understand and advance human behaviour (Goal 5).

Human behaviour and causes of behavioural responses are studied using three major levels of analyses, as outlined in general psychology:

- Biological level
- Psychological level
- Environmental level

The following section discusses how coaching psychology is guided by these psychological principles, and the extent to which all three levels of analysis are applied to maximize human potential in a coaching context.

Application of psychological principles to coaching practice

Principle 1: Behaviour is observable

A coach interacts with the coachee to observe their development during coaching sessions. For example, Shams and Lampshire (2022) reported a case study in which a coach encountered the coachee in a face-to-face situation to aid their understanding of the critical issues affecting the progress of their business. The coach in this context negotiated the intervention steps with the coachee at their desired time and space in order to apply observation techniques as well as relevant coaching tools and techniques. The following gives a brief description of the case study.

Coaching using observation techniques: an example

A family-run business was failing due to a shortage of innovative ideas and lack of advanced technology. The business took the approach of hiring two senior executives from outside the family. However, there were problems with communications and working relationships between the business and the external employees. Using relevant psychological tools, e.g. relationship mappings (diagrammatic dynamics, family sculpting and perceptual positions), the coach observed a lack of effective communication, and this was aggravated by the absence of clarity in role-specific tasks and responsibilities, decision-making and governance. These issues were discussed with the business team to accept a resolution about keeping personal preferences separate from the team business ideas and decisions. This may have helped the coach to deliver solution-focused coaching to the business (Shams and Lampshire 2022).

Principle 2: Behaviour can be measured

A coaching outcome is measured using an evaluative approach in which feedback from the coachee forms an integral part in the overall assessment. Shams and Clark (2022) discussed the value of measuring coaching outcomes to identify effect size and success factors in coaching interventions. They highlighted the importance of measuring coaching outcomes to provide significant insights into the coaching process, as well as to enhance professional practice and the personal learning of a coach.

Principle 3: Behaviour can be investigated/explored

Coaching psychology supports individuals to develop and maintain performance standards for goal attainment. In a recent review of the number of coaching research articles published in the *Journal of Applied Sport Psychology* from 1989 to 2017, Sheehy et al. (2019) discovered 690 published research articles confirming that coaching behaviour can be investigated/examined. Although the authors expressed concerns about the lack of empirical research in sports coaching, the finding indicates that coaching behaviour can be examined, explored and evaluated.

In another recent empirical literature review on the critical factors of effective coaching for early childhood educators, a rigorous search technique using A+ Education, Academic Search Complete, ERIC (EBSCO), ProQuest Education Journals, ProQuest Social Science Journals and PsychoInfo databases between March 2014 and March 2016 obtained 2630 peer-reviewed articles in English (Elek and Page 2019). This is promising in confirming that coaching psychology is the study of behavioural enquiry/investigation which requires psychological facilitation to change/modify and progress/advance. For example, one study investigated leaders' behaviour in a team meeting, using executive coaching. The findings showed that poor leadership during meetings was responsible for ineffective outcomes, and that leaders' behaviour in meetings changed significantly after coaching (Perkins 2009).

Principle 4: Behaviour can be changed/modified

This principle is mostly used in coaching psychology practice, as the main focus of a coaching intervention is to identify critical issues affecting an individual's performance to bring about positive changes in behaviour. There is a vast range of literature to substantiate this statement: for example, in a study exploring the feasibility of a coaching intervention for nursing assistants to improve communication with dementia patients, Douglas and MacPherson (2021) found that the communication of the nursing assistants improved/changed after the coaching intervention. A range of empirical research has also confirmed the effectiveness of coaching intervention in producing a change in health behaviour. The powerful influence of coaching to change and improve behavioural performance, irrespective of the mode of delivery, was confirmed in a research by Beleigoli et al. (2020). Online coaching for adults with obesity and overweight was found to be effective in increasing their engagement with a weight loss programme.

Change in behaviour is not only an individualized outcome factor from coaching; group coaching is also found to be effective for group behaviour, as was revealed by Bezner et al. (2020) with university employees. The findings of this research showed that group coaching was effective in helping to improve physical fitness and understanding of the psychology of physical activity. Coaching psychology intervention is thus widely applied to support individuals and groups. It can be expected that the application of coaching psychology practice will be extended to a wide community level, such as in school settings and community developmental programmes.

Principle 5: Behavioural outcomes can be repeated and replicated

Coaching outcomes refer to expected changes in behaviour, and these can be replicated to make further advancement in a similar situation. Shams and Clark (2022) provide critical discussion to give impetus to coaching practitioners to document their successful coaching outcomes so they can be replicated in similar coaching interventions. This will not only enhance their professional skills but also promote learning from their own coaching practice. The critical mass of coaching practice needs to be influenced by practitioners' reflective learning experiences from their coaching practice. The behaviour of both coaching practitioners and coachees can be repeated and replicated, as we see the application of similar coaching tools to the same coaching needs in the same environment. Although this may raise the question of individual differences and the various complex contextual issues affecting coaching practice despite the similar nature of coaching needs, the critical issue here is that coaching outcomes could predict the replication of the same coaching application to address similar coaching needs.

Levels of analysis in coaching psychology

This section exemplifies the three levels of analysis with relevant evidence to justify how coaching psychology is informed by psychological principles, goals and levels of analysis.

Biological level

This level aims to understand behaviour using a biological perspective, e.g. how genetics and physiology can influence human behaviour. Grant (2015) has affirmed the valuable role coaching can play as an experimental methodology to trace any changes in brain activity, highlighting the major contribution of coaching to neuroscience.

Dias et al. (2015) have called for research on the neural basis of coaching effectiveness, and the use of neuroimaging, EEG and relevant biochemical assays to develop and maintain the scientific status of evidence-based coaching practice. In my brief commentary on the lead article by Dias et al. (2015), I have argued for the need to trace the neurological basis of coaching intervention in order to make progress in understanding the effects of coaching on brain functions and cognitive processes (Shams 2015).

The neuroscience of coaching is in a promising developmental stage, with an increasing amount of empirical research in this area. For example, Boyatzis and Jack (2018) conducted experimental research, and their finding was in favour of the significant effect size of coaching on specific areas of brain function. Introducing intentional change theory, they confirmed that two different coaching approaches can activate networks and regions of the brain differently. This implies a major role of coaching to activate specific regions of the brain to function differently, which in turn causes changes in behaviour. Our brain regulates our behaviour, hence we can expect this impact of coaching on brain functions, as it involves active thinking and problem solving, reasoning and moral judgement – i.e. use of our social brain (Boyatzis and Jack 2018).

There is growing interest in aligning coaching practice with the fast-developing area of neuroscience (Bowman et al. 2013). The huge prospect of using coaching psychology to optimize performance can only be accelerated if we are proactive about applying neuroscience to coaching psychology practice.

The biological level of analysis is also applied to achieve positive health outcomes in a coaching intervention. One effective biological-level analysis in coaching psychology practice relates to health behaviour changes to obtain expected health outcomes. McGonagle et al. (2020) have found coaching is an effective intervention for alleviating burnout in research with primary care physicians. Health coaching is a popular topic in conferences, workshops and in educational programmes. This is encouraging in justifying the valuable influence of psychology in coaching in the health context. This approach to improving health and well-being using a biological level of analysis is quite often accompanied or followed by the psychological level of analysis approach. The following section aims to present a brief discussion on how the psychological level of analysis is applied in coaching practice.

Psychological level

Using mental processes and functions, this level of analysis provides a deep understanding of the causes of behavioural responses to environmental stimuli.

The application of this level is prominent in coaching psychology practice. Norman and Bober (2020) called for behavioural analysis to merge with the coaching approach to bring positive changes in health behaviour. This level of analysis is used by all coaching approaches, e.g. health coaching, sports coaching, educational coaching, etc. The primary focus is to bring positive changes in selected behavioural aspects, using the psychological level of analysis.

The psychology of coaching can be traced back to the 1940s, although the powerful underpinning of psychological theories, models and conceptual frameworks was not explicitly acknowledged at that time (Vandaveer et al. 2016). This was due to the absence of any formal accreditation process by the various professional bodies through which mandatory training and retraining can ensure an appropriate level of knowledge in psychology, and through which professional coaching practice is underpinned by psychological theories and models. There is prolific research on the use of psychological models in various areas of coaching practice in recent years, confirming the psychological level of analysis in coaching practice (McKenna and Davis 2009; Neenan and Palmer 2012). The application of this level of analysis to coaching practice is the fundamental requirement in any effective coaching practice. Lack of systematic research on the application of the psychological level of analysis may delay the legitimate status and recognition of coaching psychology as an important area of psychology. This book is expected to provide relevant knowledge and supportive resources for coaching psychology to pave the way towards psychologically informed coaching practice.

Environmental level

This level uses environmental and sociocultural issues to understand human behaviour. It overarches the biological and psychological levels of analyses and can be regarded as the context in which these two levels of analyses are applied. Good coaching practice must accompany an environmental level of analysis.

This level of analysis is often referred to as 'coaching context', and includes a multitude of contextual factors such as organizational culture, coachee and coach characteristics, coaching environment and method of delivery (Vandaveer et al. 2016). The application of environmental analysis helps us to assess the impact of a coaching intervention in diverse contexts. Using entrepreneurship as a context, Kotte et al. (2021) conducted an experiment to isolate the effect of entrepreneurship coaching to acknowledge the specific nature of coaching this entails. The application of coaching psychology cannot be completed without accounting for the environmental level of analysis. Coaching psychology explores behavioural changes caused by environmental and contextual factors.

Although all three levels of analysis are used in coaching psychology, the psychological and environmental levels are dominant in coaching practice. There is a growing interest in embracing neuroscience and biological psychology to understand changes in behaviour caused by coaching interventions. An equal representation of these three levels of analysis can ensure effective delivery of coaching psychology practice.

The application of the three levels of analysis is evident in coaching practice, hence an integrated approach using all three levels is likely to deliver the most effective coaching outcome. The three levels of analysis are complementary to each other and the presence of all three can ensure a holistic, robust approach in a coaching intervention. However, in practice, we often see the dominance of one approach – e.g. biological analysis is less prevalent than psychological analysis. This is not related to the lack of appreciation and acknowledgement of the benefits of the biological level, but the absence of empirical research and practical application of this analysis in a coaching context.

Coaching psychology is a young scientific discipline, so we can expect a more revolutionary and pragmatic approach in practice. One such approach can be an integrated analytical approach in which all three levels are used in a single coaching intervention. An example of the three levels of analysis in coaching practice is shown in the research by Jack et al. (2013). They conducted an experiment to trace the neurological basis of coaching. The biological level of analysis was employed using functional magnetic resonance imaging (fMRI); the psychological level of analysis was related to positive emotional motive attractor and negative emotional attractor; the environmental analysis in this case was the coaching context and coachee characteristics, e.g. the participants were university students. The critical issue here is that although coaching psychology research is using all three levels of analyses, this is not explicitly discussed as the focus is on the coaching processes and outcomes.

It is important to highlight the application of the three levels of analysis to establish the strong presence of psychology in all coaching practice. Figure 1.1 shows the active presence of psychological principles, goals and levels of analysis in a coaching intervention.

Figure 1.1 Psychology principles, goals and levels of analysis in coaching practice

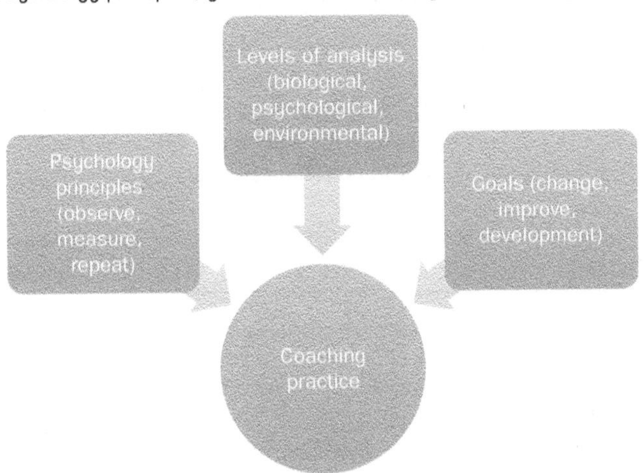

A good coaching intervention is driven by psychological principles (P) and goals (G), and applies appropriate levels of analysis (L).

Coaching psychology is firmly grounded in the behavioural sciences, and coaching psychology practice is delivered using relevant psychology key principles, goals and analysis. This means a practitioner must have relevant qualifications in a psychology subject area to train further in coaching psychology practice. Coaching psychology has now achieved formal recognition as a specialist area of psychology, and developmental work is under way for formal accreditation of coaching psychology practice. This will help coaching psychology to flourish and become popularized, and also help us to understand human behaviour from a coaching psychology perspective.

Conclusion

Coaching psychology is an important scientific, practice-based discipline to deliver knowledge of human behaviour with a focus on development and advancement, change and sustainable progress.

Vandaveer and Palmer (2016) have discussed the ongoing debate on 'where is psychology in coaching?' with the conclusion that this question has wide implications for professional practice in coaching. This is because the question has not been explored fully and the question thus remains with the growth of coaching psychology. Their call for a paradigm shift in coaching psychology to include a more contextual, holistic and dynamic approach is very appealing as this can provide the answer to the question of where psychology is in coaching. This will also help to modify the reductionist scientific framework to a broader, generalized scientific approach using the core psychological principles and contextual factors. In Chapter 4, we introduce a new psychological paradigm based on 'selective realism'.

The influence of psychology in coaching practice is undeniable. Psychological knowledge is a strong resource for a coaching practitioner to deliver effective coaching practice. Hence, a professional movement to psychologize coaching practice explicitly is needed, along with individual effort to understand, apply and evaluate psychological input in coaching practice.

References

American Psychological Association (2021) *Science of Psychology*. Available at: https://www.apa.org/action/science (accessed 9 June 2021).

Beleigoli, A., Andrade, A.Q., Diniz, M.D.F. and Ribeiro, A.L. (2010) Personalized web-based weight loss behaviour change program with and without dietitian online coaching for adults with overweight and obesity: Randomized controlled trial, *Journal of Medical Internet Research*, 22(11): e17494.

Bezner, J.R., Franklin, K.A., Lloyd, L.K. and Crixell, S.H. (2020) Effect of group health behaviour change coaching on psychosocial constructs associated with physical activity among university employees, *International Journal of Sport and Exercise Psychology*, 18(1): 93–107.

Bowman, M., Ayers, K.M., King, J.C. and Page, L.J. (2013) The neuroscience of coaching, in J. Passmore, D.B. Peterson and T. Freire (eds) *The Wiley-Blackwell Handbook of the Psychology of Coaching and Mentoring*. Oxford: Wiley-Blackwell, pp. 89–111.

Boyatzis, R.E. and Jack, A.I. (2018) The neuroscience of coaching, *Consulting Psychology Journal: Practice and Research*, 70(1): 11–27.

Dias, P.G., Palmer, S., O'Riordan, S., de Freitas, B.S., Bevalaqua, N.C.M. and Nardi, E.A. (2015) Perspectives and challenges for the study of brain responses to coaching: Enhancing the dialogue between the fields of neuroscience and coaching psychology, *The Coaching Psychologist*, 11(1): 11–17.

Douglas, N.F. and MacPherson, M.K. (2021) Positive changes in certified nursing assistants' communication behaviours with people with dementia: Feasibility of a coaching strategy, *American Journal of Speech-Language Pathology*, 30(1): 239–52.

Elek, C. and Page, J. (2019) Critical features of effective coaching for early childhood educators: A review of empirical research literature, *Professional Development in Education*, 45(4): 567–85.

Grant, A. (2015) Coaching the brain: Neuroscience or neuro-nonsense?, *The Coaching Psychologist*, 11(1): 21–7.

Holt, N., Bremner, A., Sutherland, E., Vliek, M., Passer, M. and Smith, R. (2019) *Psychology: The Science of Mind and Behaviour*, 4th edn. London: McGraw-Hill Education.

Jack, A.I., Boyatzis, R.E., Khawaja, M.S., Passarelli, A.M. and Leckie, R.L. (2013) Visioning in the brain: An fMRI study of inspirational coaching and mentoring, *Social Neuroscience*, 8(4): 369–84.

Kotte, S., Diermann, I., Rosing, K. and Möller, H. (2021) Entrepreneur coaching: A two-dimensional framework in context, *Applied Psychology: An International Review*, 70(2): 518–55.

McGonagle, A.K., Schwab, L., Yahanda, N. et al. (2020) Coaching for primary care physician well-being: A randomized trial and follow-up analysis, *Journal of Occupational Health Psychology*, 25(5): 297–314.

McKenna, D. and Davis, S. (2009) Hidden in plain sight: The active ingredients of executive coaching, *Industrial and Organizational Psychology: Perspectives on Science and Practice, 2(3)*: 244–60.

Neenan, M. and Palmer, S. (2012) *Cognitive Behavioural Coaching in Practice: An Evidence Based Approach, Essential Coaching Skills and Knowledge*. New York: Routledge.

Normand, M.P. and Bober, J. (2020) Health coaching by behaviour analysts in practice: How and why, *Behaviour Analysis: Research and Practice*, 20(2): 108–19.

Perkins, R.D. (2009) How executive coaching can change leader behaviour and improve meeting effectiveness: An exploratory study, *Consulting Psychology Journal: Practice and Research*, 61(4): 298–318.

Shams, M. (2015) Why is it important to understand the neurological basis of coaching intervention?, *The Coaching Psychologist*, 11(1): 28–9.

Shams, M. (2022) *Supporting the Family Business: A Coaching Practitioner's Handbook*, 2nd edn. New York: Routledge.

Shams, M. and Clark, G. (2022) Learning and developing skills from coaching outcomes, in M. Shams, *Supporting the Family Business: A Coaching Practitioner's Handbook*, 2nd edn. New York: Routledge, pp. 82–103.

Shams, M. and Lampshire, J. (2022) Group dynamics in family business: A focused, integrated and inclusive coaching approach, in M. Shams, *Supporting the Family Business: A Coaching Practitioner's Handbook*, 2nd edn. New York: Routledge, pp. 41–61.

Sheehy, T.L., Dieffenbach, K. and Reed, P. (2019) An exploration of coaching research in *Journal of Applied Sport Psychology* from 1989 to 2017, *Journal of Applied Sport Psychology*, 31(3): 352–65.

Vandaveer, V.V., Lowman, R.L., Pearlman, K.P. and Brannick, J.P. (2016) A practice analysis of coaching psychology: Toward a foundational competency model, *Consulting Psychology Journal: Practice and Research Special Issue: International Perspectives on Becoming a Master Coaching Psychologist*, 68(2): 118–42.

Vandaveer, V.V. and Palmer, S. (2016) International perspectives on becoming a master coaching psychologist, *Consulting Psychology Journal: Practice and Research*, 68(2): 99–104.

2 Understanding coaching practice from a psychological perspective

Manfusa Shams

Summary

The need for a solid theoretical foundation of coaching psychology and the demands for theory-driven coaching practice are generating critical issues influencing the development of coaching psychology as a distinctive branch of applied and practice-based psychology.

This chapter presents the theoretical basis of coaching psychology and the practical application of theories relevant to coaching practice. The discussion addresses the key questions of how coaching psychology knowledge is constructed, and how coaching practice is developed and delivered, using a few selected psychological schools of thought.

Keywords: coaching psychology, differential coaching practice, holism, local and global practice, professional coaching practice.

Introduction

The fundamental knowledge on which coaching psychology is grounded is derived from the concept of 'developing individuals' on a continuum of life span. Individuals have the capabilities to change their behaviour with support from an appropriate coaching intervention. Using a coaching practitioner's relevant support, individuals drive their own behaviour to reach their desired goals. The influence of coaching is evident in the behavioural transformation of the coachee. During this transformational journey, an individual may face various constraints and challenges. A coaching practitioner provides the support to meet those challenges, to overcome any constraints, and to excel in their performance for goal attainment. There is, however, no restriction imposed by a coach on the timeline of the journey, except that the coach inspires and facilitates the process to achieve the desired goal using the individual's own response repertoire. An individual is thus able to gain positive outcomes from the coaching intervention using their own personal resources and innate abilities to make changes for further progress. A coaching psychology practitioner is thus an enabler, facilitator and motivator.

A discipline has a theoretical ground, and the emergence of a discipline is guided by the selected primary theoretical constructs. Coaching is strongly grounded in psychology, and coaching psychology is emerging as a fine tuned discipline in its own right, despite the strong influence of a few psychological schools of thought, such as positive psychology and humanistic psychology. The developmental journey, along with highlights of the practical side of this discipline, is presented in this chapter.

Aims

The main aim of this chapter is to critically discuss key issues of professional practice in coaching psychology. The discussion focuses on the psychological constructs underpinning coaching practice, and the influence of selected schools of thought on developing the knowledge of coaching psychology. It also looks at how coaching practice is informed by these schools of thought.

The chapter presents evidence-based discussion on the significant contribution of coaching psychology to enhancing theoretical knowledge in psychology as well as the practical application of psychological knowledge, with a focus on coaching psychology practice.

The theoretical underpinning of coaching psychology practice

The term 'coach' has been used in various forms since the eighteenth century. The popular usage was for a person responsible for guiding a carriage: the driver of a horse-drawn carriage was called a coach at that time. Stacy (2014) used a popular joke that most history teachers in the USA are called coaches, and the term coach is naturally assigned to teachers without any knowledge of the teachers that they are regarded as a coach. There was an increasing use of the term coach in association with sports during the early nineteenth century, although it is also used in various forms in the education and sports sectors in different countries – e.g. in the Indian subcontinent a popular term for a coach was 'sardar' ('captain', 'head', 'guru') to refer to the leader who brings changes to the group's performance. However, this role-related behaviour was not the behaviour that 'coach' implies in the present-day context.

During the Industrial Revolution in the early decades of the twentieth century, in the era of advanced technological invention, industrial needs were extended to include personal management, consulting and counselling to increase output and enhance behavioural performance. Coaching practice was not recognized at that time. The influence of different schools of thought dominated the science of human behaviour from the early nineteenth century. Since then, psychology has been one of the most developed strongly rooted scientific disciplines with the capacity to evolve in relation to the increasing demands of the environment in which individuals live. Coaching is fundamentally a psychology-driven practice ensuring spontaneous growth and development in a supportive environment. Coaching practice is a personalized and non-directive engagement with the coachee (Passmore et al. 2021). This approach in coaching practice meets the needs of diverse population groups because of the attention to the personal needs of a coachee. The personalized approach in coaching practice has helped to broaden the application of coaching psychology to all across society.

The following section discusses the influence of relevant schools of thought in psychology on the formation of coaching psychology knowledge. It highlights both the theoretical foundation of coaching psychology as well as practical application of the knowledge gained from these schools of thought to inform effective coaching practice.

The influence of psychological schools of thought on coaching psychology

The early schools of thought during the period 1832–1920 were structuralism and functionalism. Structuralism refers to the analysis of the elements of mind at a basic level, and functionalism focused on the functional aspects of consciousness. There have been a lot of changes in theorizing human behaviour since these early schools: e.g. learning and experiences, environmental influences, consciousness and thinking, self-actualization/fulfilment, innate ability to change, etc., were considered important to understand individuals' and groups' behaviour. The respective schools of thought representing these areas are behaviourism, cognitive behaviourism, humanistic and positive psychology.

However, these schools of thoughts (structuralism and functionalism) were not excluded completely. Rather, they are still considered as the root of psychology as a scientific discipline. In addition, functionalism is thought to have influenced the development of cognitive psychology (mental processes) and evolutionary psychology which studies behavioural adaptation. The most recent schools of thought are behaviourism, cognitive, humanistic, psychodynamic and neuroscience, and positive psychology (Feldman 2020).

The next section presents the schools of thought that have contributed to the constructive development of coaching psychology knowledge. It asserts that coaching is a psychology-informed practice, hence coaching psychology is a valuable branch of the psychology discipline.

Schools of thought

Behaviourism

This school of thought, proposed by John B. Watson in 1913, was a breakthrough in understanding human behaviour, with an emphasis on the environmental influences on human behaviour, particularly the powerful role of learning to shape experiences and behavioural outcomes. During the 1930s B.F. Skinner offered explanations to understand behaviour using reinforcement and environmental stimuli to effect changes in behaviour. Skinner emphasized exploring causes and consequences of behaviour.

Coaching psychology uses behavioural observation to support coachees' development in relation to their environment.

Cognitive

Human thinking processes, particularly information processing and brain functions regulating our thinking, are the primary focus of this school (Hermann Ebbinghaus in the late eighteenth century, and the most influential gestalt psychology proposed by Max Wertheimer, Wolfgang Köhler and Kurt Koffka in the 1920s). The direct influence of this school on generating coaching psychology knowledge cannot be established, although there are coaching tools based on their ideas, e.g. the cognitive behavioural coaching technique (Minzlaff 2019). There is a growing body of literature to confirm the effectiveness of cognitive behavioural coaching, which aims to modify beliefs and support cognitive development to improve performance. Grant (2017) has described cognitive behavioural coaching as derived from cognitive behavioural theory to facilitate goal attainment and changing reciprocal relationships between the environment and individuals' thoughts, feelings and behaviour. The influence of this school of thought is to provide a promising advance in the use of cognitive theories and models in a coaching context.

Humanistic

The humanistic school of thought focuses on human potential, growth and self-actualization. The emphasis is on the development of the whole 'self', which is linked to finding one's authentic self (Gregory and Levy 2012). This school of thought has the most influence on the development of coaching psychology. The humanistic perspective suggests that all individuals have the natural capacity to grow, develop and change their behaviour. As such, individuals are capable of reaching their full potential, implying that inner strength can be reinforced with the application of coaching. Coaching focuses on human growth and change. The influence of humanistic psychology on the construction of coaching psychology knowledge is undeniable. Grounded on Carl Rogers' person-centred theory and Abraham Maslow's self-actualization principle, the humanistic approach promotes the self-sustaining and innate abilities of individuals to grow to their full potential.

Although the humanistic perspective appears to have had a strong influence on the construction of coaching psychology knowledge and practice-related delivery techniques, however, not all psychological constructs underpinning coaching practice have been derived from all aspects of the humanistic school of thought. For example, one of the principal features of humanistic psychology is that individuals have a strong experiential orientation. This feature is not the central focus in coaching psychology as the emphasis is on supporting an individual's personal growth and development, live and at the present time, with or without the use of their past experiences exclusively. Nevertheless, the humanistic model is focused on the total development of an individual, and this brings this theoretical model close to coaching psychology practice (Cassidy 2010).

Coaching psychology is a scientific discipline on its own merits. Denial of the influence of dominant schools of thought may be difficult, yet this is desirable to achieve the theoretical development of psychology in coaching and professional practice in coaching psychology. Lyle (2010) has warned against the blanket use of humanistic principles in coaching, as coaching practice is context-specific. The humanistic perspective mainly provides the philosophical ground for coaching psychology to develop effective practice. Coaching psychology is essentially a diversion from the main psychology root with all other branches around it. The diversity in coaching psychology practice supports the valuable contributions of different schools of thought. Hence the humanistic perspective can be more influential for one coaching approach than others, e.g. for health coaching rather than sports coaching. It is essential to explore the influence of other disciplines on coaching psychology to have a good understanding of how they have influenced the development of coaching psychology as a distinctive practice-based discipline. The most recent call for moving beyond humanistic psychology is diverting the attention of aspiring coaching practitioners towards a more dynamic and pragmatic positive psychology and progressive coaching psychology (Cassidy 2010).

Positive psychology

As a process of natural progress in theorizing coaching practice, positive psychology provides a refreshing and revolutionary platform to advance coaching psychology. Although the central tenets of humanistic psychology are prevalent in positive psychology, the principles are more refined and repurposed to suit the needs of coaching psychology practice. The practice of positive psychology has provided the groundwork for coaching psychology to emerge as a discipline driven by psychological principles. Positive psychology provides a backbone to coaching psychology. A solid theoretical and evidence-based groundwork is essential for coaching psychology to establish itself as a scientific discipline (Seligman 2007). The popular positive psychology coaching practice is valuable in achieving effective coaching outcomes (Susing et al. 2011; Passmore and Oades 2014; Sims 2017). The concept of 'optimum human functioning' in positive psychology is aligned with the two key principles of coaching psychology – change and growth. These are the key ingredients of human functioning to achieve the optimum level of performance. The fine line between positive psychology and coaching psychology is that, unlike positive psychology, coaching psychology is essentially a practice-based discipline with a focus on developing individuals using their own potential, and it is still evolving. Grant and Atad (2021) conducted a comparative study on coaching psychology intervention vs positive psychology intervention using training programmes in these two areas with postgraduate university students. Their findings confirmed the distinction between these two disciplines, with significantly better outcomes for coaching psychology intervention than for positive psychology intervention. This relates to goal attainment, self-awareness/insight, well-being and solution-focused thinking. Noteworthy is the solution-focused coaching technique applied for coaching psychology intervention which can be used to enhance personal agency, and is more attuned to personal development and progress in performance. This is unique to coaching psychology practice and distinguishes coaching psychology from positive psychology.

The immense benefit of selected schools of thought for coaching psychology practice is that coaching psychology is accompanied by a strong set of discipline-based knowledge, and practice is informed by pre-existing knowledge from these disciplines. Hence the issues of reliability and validity in coaching practice are addressed appropriately through these disciplines' contributions to coaching psychology knowledge construction. Coaching does not exist in a vacuum and must have a strong theoretical foundation to deliver effective practice. The absence of coaching psychology theories is caused by attention being diverted to developing coaching practices using relevant schools of thought as discussed above, rather than developing thoughtful discussion on the psychological constructs underpinning effective coaching practice, and theoretical grounds on which coaching psychology knowledge is delivered for practice.

Since the introduction of the GROW model of coaching in the 1980s (Whitmore 2009), with wide acceptance of this model as an effective business coaching model, a series of theoretical models have been developed to support coaching practice in specific areas. For example, Grant (2011) offered the RE-GROW model as a variation of the GROW model to provide depth in understanding the nature of coaching sessions as determinants of coaching efficacy. This model has focused on review and evaluation of each coaching session to ensure coaching engagement. Other frequently cited models of coaching are PRACTICE (Palmer 2008), the ABCDEF model (Ellis et al. 1997), the integrative coaching model (Williams et al. 2011), and the developmental model (Laske 1999). These models are concerned with the delivery of effective coaching practice. The critical issue is how knowledge of coaching psychology was generated in order to develop the discipline. Also what ensures effective coaching practice delivery using appropriate theoretical knowledge?

The discussion on selected relevant schools of thought indicates that the theoretical ground of coaching psychology is still not fully developed. This is to be expected as coaching psychology is emerging as a practice-based scientific discipline and it still has not quite achieved maturity in terms of a grounded discipline. It is important to continue discussion and professional work to develop its theoretical basis. To facilitate the process, a community of coaching practice can ensure the initiative to provide the solid theoretical grounding of coaching psychology (Shams 2013).

Understanding coaching psychology practice

Coaching practice is driven by psychology principles and knowledge, and the practice is delivered to a non-clinical population to enhance functioning in a particular context. The significant feature of coaching psychology practice is the application to a non-clinical population. This leads to the important issue about the differences between coaching practices and other practices for which the target group also belongs to a non-clinical population.

This section presents a comparative account of different coaching practices, along with the major distinctions compared to a few relevant disciplinary practices.

What is coaching psychology practice?

Coaching psychology practice refers to psychology knowledge delivery from a coaching perspective. The primary focus is on applying relevant psychology knowledge to optimize human performance. The application and practice are two key drivers here as knowledge is applied to a practice, and a practice in turn is advancing knowledge. The reciprocal positive relationship between application and practice is a key characteristic of coaching psychology.

The main features of coaching psychology practice are:

- Maximizing human potential
- Personal growth and self-directed learning
- Solution-focused and performance enhancement
- Facilitator for goal attainments (Shams 2022).

Each of these features is manifested in the expected behavioural change. There has been an increasing interest in coaching psychology practice (Mennin et al. 2013). This could be credited to the growing success of coaching interventions for making a change in behaviour to reach the optimum level of performance. Interest is generated to understand how coaching practice is underpinned by psychological constructs. Coaching practice itself was instrumental in gaining the formal recognition for coaching psychology as a specialist psychology subject area. The critical issue here is that coaching is also considered as a method to improve performance (Gentry et al. 2013). It can also be an application tool: as such, coaching psychology is exclusively an applied and practice-based scientific discipline. The debate on coaching as a method vs practice continues. This is because practice itself is a methodological procedure. The published research evidence uses 'coaching method' and 'coaching practices' interchangeably, although there is a fine distinctive line between these two terms – a method is a technique, and a practice is a delivery approach using a technique/several techniques. The nature of the delivery depends on the type(s) of technique(s) and this makes coaching psychology a distinctive practice.

Major features of coaching psychology practice

The fundamental issue of coaching psychology in practice is the application of relevant coaching tools and techniques, psychometric tests and other relevant developmental measures in a non-clinical context. Hence, knowledge of psychological measures and psychometric tools, administration capabilities and skills, interpretation of scores, outcomes and ethical issues is essential for effective coaching practice to facilitate and enhance human functioning. From this perspective, coaching psychology practice is different from other practices, such as counselling and clinical psychology, medical and allied health practices. The following sections provide a brief comparative account of coaching and counselling psychology practices, coaching and clinical psychology practices, and differential coaching practices.

Coaching psychology and counselling psychology practice

Coaching and counselling psychology practices share similar critical issues in relation to the application of psychological knowledge to their respective practices. This relates to supporting individuals to improve their present. Coaching was used in various organizations during the 1940s, although the term used was consulting rather than coaching (Hart et al. 2001). Coaching psychology was not fully developed as a practice to support human growth and development until the 1980s. However, it emerged as a method rather than a fully grown scientific discipline driven by relevant psychological principles (Grant 2016). Similarly, counselling was increasingly in use after the Second World War following from Carl Rogers' seminal work on counselling (Gladding 1996). The meeting point of these two disciplines is the focus on 'behavioural change' (Hart et al. 2001), however, they differ in the delivery of practice and population groups (Grant and Green 2018). Coaching psychology practice is engaged with non-clinical individuals and groups, whereas counselling psychology practice is not necessarily limited to the non-clinical. Usually counselling psychology deals with past events to make a change in the present, but coaching psychology practice focuses on the real-time live presence within a defined context. Counselling psychology was developed rapidly using different schools of thought, such as the psychodynamic school of thought (Kohut 1977). As such, both coaching and counselling share the same developmental line prior to emerging as a scientific psychology discipline.

Coaching psychology practice is a co-creative process in which the coach and coachee have an equal partnership to achieve the expected coaching outcomes. Coaching practice is more action-oriented with positive steps, and is grounded on defined goals/achievements. Counselling psychology practice aims to untangle complex past experiences, with a focus on applying relevant therapeutic interventions. The individuals under counselling are usually less active recipients at the start of counselling, and rely on counselling psychologists' direct or non-directive guidance to solve problems, although there are variations in counselling practices. Coachees are usually active agents making changes in their lives, hence the present rather than the past dominates the coaching psychology practice.

We have seen an increasing number of counselling psychologists engage in coaching practice, with the vision to practise coaching outside therapeutic influences. Counselling psychologists' interest in moving over to coaching psychology practice indicates the immense value inherent in the application and practice of coaching psychology.

Coaching and clinical psychology practice

The main difference between clinical and coaching psychology practice is that clinical psychology is focused on serving clinical population groups who may or may not have exhibited mild to severe mental health difficulties and behavioural disorders, but for whom relevant assessments and diagnosis leading to treatment options are required. Coaching psychology practice does not involve clinical diagnosis and treatment, and this makes a solid boundary between coaching and clinical psychology. Clinical psychologists are required to complete formal British Psychological Society accreditation qualifications and training. They are trained to reduce psychological distress, and to enhance and promote psychological well-being using the systematic application of knowledge derived from psychological theory and research (the British Psychological Society 2019). At the time of writing this book in 2021, coaching psychology practice is working to achieve this accreditation status from the British Psychological Society in the UK.

The common features in both clinical and coaching psychology practice are that both are practice-based disciplines grounded on relevant psychological knowledge, models and theories. However, clinical psychology practice has more depth in application to alleviate psychological distress, emotional and behavioural problems, and has a far-reaching goal. Thus the application of the clinical intervention goes beyond benefitting the individual or group, to apply to institutional and community levels of health and social care, such as the NHS, the third sector, independent providers, inpatients and community, primary, secondary and tertiary care, and with all age groups (the British Psychological Society 2019). Coaching psychology practice is also applied to benefit group and institutional performances, and behavioural changes, however, these are aimed to benefit individuals and groups from non-clinical population groups in a particular setting, e.g. the NHS and social care leaders (NHS 2021).

The application of coaching psychology is now extended to health care (Wang et al. 2016). One example is the NHS England leadership programme. This relates to providing an extra layer of learning experience through coaching to optimize learning experiences, and growing deep insights into personal developmental needs.

The value of coaching psychology practice for crisis and challenging situations is enormous as leaders are able to improve their communications and decision-making through conversations with the coach, and using reflection as a method to evaluate their own performance. Coaching psychology in practice is progressing fast to demonstrate the immense value in its practical application for individuals' and society's performance and management, development and maintenance, communication and interpersonal relations as well as national and global levels of decision-making, collaboration and production. Coaching psychology practice is varied and context-specific. The next section presents a brief overview of differential coaching psychology practice.

Differential coaching psychology practice

Coaching psychology practice is delivered in a particular context with a focus on facilitating an individual's behavioural progression and performance enhancement. It aims to support an individual with full consideration of the context in which the individual is living. For example, a business leader's need for coaching is influenced by their performance in a business (Shams 2022). A business context needs to be aligned with the most appropriate coaching intervention. Similarly, a group coaching intervention is determined by the nature of the group and the group's functions. An example is group coaching for a sports team, and sport provides the context here.

The context and needs of the individuals and groups determine the application of different types of coaching practices underpinned by different psychological schools of thought (Castiello D'Antonio 2018) to achieve positive coaching outcomes (Shams and Clark 2022). The main differential coaching psychology practices are developmental, behavioural, cognitive behavioural, existential, psychodynamic, gestalt and psychoanalytic (Castiello D'Antonio 2018). Coaching psychology practices are also designated according to their approaches, for example, a narrative approach in coaching, positive psychological approaches in coaching, evidence-based coaching, the gestalt approach, or motivational interviewing (Passmore et al. 2012). However, the common psychological construct running through all these coaching deliveries is 'developing individuals'. Coaching psychology facilitates the process of developing individuals to achieve optimum performance using their full potential.

The powerful influence of differential coaching psychology on individuals at different levels and on society's functions is increasingly valued and recognized. Coaching psychology practice is bridging the gap between theory and practice as it applies relevant theoretical knowledge to practice. The next section summarizes the theoretical and practical contributions of coaching psychology.

The contribution of coaching psychology to society

Coaching is not a localized practice. On the contrary, coaching is a practice which has been prevalent in all societies since the 1930s–1940s. However, coaching practice was not regulated by psychological discipline at that time, so coaching psychology was not actually in practice to benefit society. It was during the 1980s that coaching psychology emerged as a unique scientific discipline with a powerful influence on changing individual and group behaviour, organizational changes and role-specific behavioural functions, such as leadership.

Theoretical contributions

Coaching psychology is developing fast with a focus on practical applications, hence the theoretical underpinning of coaching practice is still reliant on the existing psychological schools of thought, such as positive psychology, humanistic psychology and existential psychology. However, there has been increasing interest in grounding coaching psychology on various theoretical constructs, models and frameworks (Passmore et al. 2012; Shams 2022). These initiatives to offer theoretical models are expected to facilitate the development of relevant theories unique to coaching psychology practice, although the main theoretical construct will remain the same. This is to support individuals and groups to change, develop and grow their full potential, and to help maintain a sustainable progression.

The theoretical advancement of psychological knowledge from the coaching psychology discipline is focused on integrated knowledge about human developmental processes which can be shaped, modified and driven by individuals themselves using their own abilities and potential. Chapter 4 proposes a coaching practitioner's model in which we discuss the key elements of individuals' drivers to develop, modify and grow their own behavioural functions, and cognitive enhancement in relation to their environment. We also offer a new psychology paradigm embracing coaching psychology which can also be a landmark to start a journey for the development of this theoretical strand with potential for enormous benefits for individuals and groups around the globe.

Practical applications of coaching psychology knowledge

The practical application of psychology knowledge in coaching practice is immense. Coaching psychology is a practice-based discipline which has an exclusive application of psychological principles to make a change in individual and group behaviour in a non-clinical context. It is offering solution-focused interventions for individuals and groups to change/amend and develop their behaviour specific to their own needs. Individuals are the active agents to make a change and to accept the change as a result of coaching intervention.

The practical contributions of coaching psychology practice can be located in both a local and global context. The unique feature of this contribution is that the application is uniformly applied to all, irrespective of cultural diversity and differences in geographical location, although cultural context may need to be taken into consideration. For example, leadership coaching applies relevant coaching tools and techniques to all leaders uniformly as it is the role-specific behaviour that needs the coaching practitioner's attention. The fundamental issue is that 'leadership behaviour' should be governed by leadership style, interpersonal relations with employees and the related environment. Coaching psychology interventions are thus not limited to a local context but have a far-reaching influence on a global level. An example of a localized coaching intervention is for school education in a city, and for global coaching, examples are coaching practice to global leaders from a large business organization, or sports coaching for international football teams (Robinson 2014). The major issue is the practical value of coaching psychology beyond the individual level to group and community levels (Shams 2013). It is expected that the application of coaching psychology will grow with the various environmental challenges society is continually facing, and the increasingly complex demands on individuals as they strive to achieve competitive advantage in their behavioural performance.

Conclusion

Coaching psychology practice is characterized by change, development and enhancement. Using a holistic approach, the fundamental construct in coaching psychology practice is 'whole' or 'total'. This discipline-focused practice is delivered in a 'real-life' context, and as such it is continuously evolving (Grant 2016). The solid theoretical foundation of coaching psychology is developing fast using evidence-based research and practice-driven knowledge. Coaching psychology is opening up a new era to understand human behaviour and to support individuals' development using the most natural approach, in which individuals are the active agents of their own change and progress.

References

BPS (British Psychological Society) (2019) *Standards for the Accreditation of Doctoral Programmes in Clinical Psychology*. Leicester: BPS.

Cassidy, T. (2010) Holism in sports coaching: Beyond humanistic psychology, *International Journal of Sports Science & Coaching*, 5(4): 439–43.

Castiello D'Antonio, A. (2018) Coaching psychology and positive psychology in work and organizational psychology, *The Psychologist-Manager Journal*, 21(2): 130–50.

Ellis, A., Gordon, J., Neenan, M. and Palmer, S. (1997) *Stress Counselling: A Rational Emotive Behaviour Approach*. London: Cassell.

Feldman, S. (2020) *Psychology and Your Life*, 4th edn. New York: McGraw-Hill Education.

Gentry, W.A., Manning, L., Wolf, A.K., Hernez-Broome, G., and Allen, L.W. (2013) What coaches believe are best practices for coaching: A qualitative study of interviews from coaches residing in Asia and Europe, *Journal of Leadership Studies*, 7(2): 18–31.

Gladding, S.T. (1996) *Counseling: A Comprehensive Profession*. New York: Pearson.

Grant, A.M. (2011) Is it time to REGROW the GROW model? Issues related to teaching coaching session structures, *The Coaching Psychologist*, 7(2): 118–26.

Grant, A. (2016) What can Sydney tell us about coaching? Research with implications for practice from down under, *Consulting Psychology Journal: Practice and Research*, 68(2): 105–17.

Grant, A.M. (2017) Solution-focused cognitive-behavioural coaching for sustainable high performance and circumventing stress, fatigue, and burnout, *Consulting Psychology Journal: Practice and Research*, Special issue: Fatigue in the Workplace, 69(2): 98–111.

Grant, A. and Atad, O. (2021) Coaching psychology interventions vs positive psychology interventions: The measurable benefits of a coaching relationship, *The Journal of Positive Psychology*, 1(18): 1–13.

Grant, M.A. and Green, R.M. (2018) Developing clarity on the coaching–counselling conundrum: Implications for counsellors and psychotherapists, *Counselling and Psychotherapy Research*, 18(4): 347–55.
Gregory, B.J. and Levy, E.P. (2012) Humanistic/person-centered approaches, in D.B. Peterson and T. Freire (eds) *The Wiley-Blackwell Handbook of the Psychology of Coaching and Mentoring*. Oxford: Wiley-Blackwell, pp. 283–97.
Hart, V., Blattner, J. and Leipsic, S. (2001) Coaching versus therapy: A perspective, *Consulting Psychology Journal*, 53(4): 229–37.
Kohut, H. (1977) *Analysis of the Self*. New York: International Universities Press.
Laske, O.E. (1999) An integrated model of developmental coaching, *Consulting Psychology Journal: Practice and Research*, 51(3): 139–59.
Lyle, J. (2010) Holism in sports coaching: Beyond humanistic psychology: A commentary, *International Journal of Sports Science & Coaching*, 5(4): 449–52.
Mennin, D.S., Ellard, K.K., Fresco, D.M. and Gross, J.J. (2013) United we stand: Emphasizing commonalities across cognitive-behavioural therapies, *Behaviour Therapy*, 44(2): 234–48.
Minzlaff, K.A. (2019) Organisational coaching: Integrating motivational interviewing and mindfulness with cognitive behavioural coaching, *Coaching: An International Journal of Theory, Research and Practice*, 12(1): 15–28.
NHS (2021) Coaching and mentoring for leaders, NHS website. Available at: https://people.nhs.uk/support-for-leaders/coaching-and-mentoring-for-leaders/ (accessed 27 July 2021).
Palmer, S. (2008) The PRACTICE model of coaching: Towards a solution-focused approach, *Coaching Psychology International*, 1(1): 4–8.
Passmore, J., Liu, W. and Tewald, S. (2021) Future trends in coaching: Results from a global coach survey, *The Coaching Psychologist*, 17(2): 41–52.
Passmore, J. and Oades, L.G. (2014) Positive psychology coaching: A model for coaching practice, *The Coaching Psychologist*, 10(2): 68–70.
Passmore, J., Peterson, B.D. and Freire, T. (eds) (2012) *The Wiley-Blackwell Handbook of the Psychology of Coaching and Mentoring*. Oxford: Wiley-Blackwell.
Robinson, P.E. (2014) *Foundations of Sports Coaching*, 2nd edn. London: Routledge [online].
Seligman, P.M. (2007) Coaching and positive psychology, *Australian Psychologist*, 42(4): 266–7.
Shams, M. (2013) Communities of coaching practice: Developing a new approach, *International Coaching Psychology Review*, 8(2): 89–91.
Shams, M. (2022) *Supporting the Family Business: A Coaching Practitioner's Handbook*, 2nd edn. New York: Routledge.
Shams, M. and Clark, G. (2022) Learning and developing skills from coaching outcomes, in M. Shams, *Supporting the Family Business: A Coaching Practitioner's Handbook*, 2nd edn. New York: Routledge, pp. 81–103.
Sims, C. (2017) Second wave positive psychology coaching with difficult emotions: Introducing the mnemonic of 'TEARS HOPE', *The Coaching Psychologist*, 13(2): 66–78.
Stacy, M. (2014) The historical origins of social studies teacher as athletic coach, *American Educational History Journal*, 41(1–2): 301–12.
Susing, I., Green, S. and Grant, A.M. (2011) The potential use of the Authenticity Scale as an outcome measure in executive coaching, *The Coaching Psychologist*, 7(1): 16–25.
Wang, Q., Li, H., Pang, W., Liang, S. and Su, W. (2016) Developing an integrated framework of problem-based learning and coaching psychology for medical education: A participatory research, *BMC Medical Education*, 16(2): 2–20.

Whitmore, J. (2009) *Coaching for Performance: GROWing Human Potential and Purpose: The Principles and Practice of Coaching and Leadership*, 4th edn. London: Nicholas Brealey Publishing.

Williams, H., Palmer, S. and Wallace, E. (2011) An integrative coaching approach for family businesses, in M. Shams and D. Lane (eds) *Coaching in the Family Owned Business: A Path to Growth*. New York: Routledge, pp. 21–40.

Coaching psychology as a profession: Ethical and practice-related issues

Andrea Giraldez-Hayes and Wendy-Ann Smith

Summary

Coaching is an age-old profession, with coaching psychology emerging as a distinct domain of psychology in 2000. Coaching psychology is grounded in the science of human behaviour, with the practice of this science known as evidenced-based coaching. It largely remains unregulated, as does coaching. The training and ethical development of coaching psychologists require studies in higher institutions – it would be misleading to consider coaching psychology practice as a coaching practice, offered by a coach without any regulated formal professional qualification in psychology. It is argued that the difference is in the unobservable: that is, the use of science and the well-grounded ethical training inherent in the practice of a coaching psychologist. An outline of the various ethical codes in coaching, the ethical considerations in the boundaries of coaching and therapy, and the need for clear contracting are explored in this chapter. Additionally, the tension felt by a coaching psychologist in a largely unregulated profession is discussed, with case studies and reflective questions.

Keywords: ethical guidelines, ethics in coaching psychology, coaching psychology practice, ethical codes, professional issues in coaching.

Introduction

Anthony Grant (2008: 23) defined coaching psychology as the 'systematic application of behavioural science [within a coaching context] to the enhancement of life experience, work performance and well-being of individuals, groups and organizations'. Calls have been made to recast coaching psychology as a separate domain of study, parallel to occupational, health or forensic psychology (Passmore and Lai 2019). Passmore (2021) suggests that while there are few observable differences between coaching and coaching psychology, the study of psychology can enhance practice, and may lead to materially different outcomes. Atad et al. (2021) propose that an understanding of the science of human change, personality, motivation and strengths born from psychology is fundamental to effective coaching. Recently, they have argued for a simplified definition of coaching psychology, in that '*Coaching Psychology is simply the science of human emotion, cognition and behaviour (i.e. psychology) that underpins coaching practice*' (Atad et al. 2021: 44). And they define the application of coaching psychology in coaching practice – evidenced-based coaching (EBC) – as the 'applied arm of Coaching Psychology, which draws on the best current knowledge of theory, research and practice from scientific domains of psychology, education and business management to coaching practice' (Atad et al. 2021: 44). At the heart of effective coaching and coaching psychology is ethical decision-making guided by morals, values and ethical guidelines. This chapter discusses the what, who and how of a coaching psychologist, and explores the ethical and professional accountabilities and challenges in maintaining integrity of practice.

What and who is a coaching psychologist?

There are different types of practising coaching psychologist. Some had their initial training in the clinical-therapeutic domain, in occupational psychology, sports psychology or other specific areas and have taken the mandated training to be formally registered as a chartered psychologist. Others have completed an undergraduate degree in psychology. In both cases, psychologists can train to become coaches, either through a coaching training school or specifically studying coaching psychology, often through a postgraduate university masters course. A second route is those who have a full undergraduate or postgraduate degree in another discipline, who may or may not have undertaken coaching training, and then completed a masters in coaching psychology.

While the title of 'psychologist' is mostly a legally protected title in many countries, for example, Australia, France and the United States of America, this protection is not afforded to the use of 'coaching psychologist'. Some practitioners use the title of psychologist in various forms – for example, coaching psychologist, positive psychologist – and this is an issue that causes tension among practising professionals, due to the lack of clarity as to what it means to the public, for accountability and the training requirements.

Although there is not a clear pathway to become a coaching psychologist, recently, after many years of work, the British Psychological Society (BPS) has allowed the creation of the Division of Coaching Psychology. According to the new regulations, graduates in psychology who have Graduate Basis for Chartered Membership (achieved after completing at least a 2:2 on an undergraduate honours degree), or have completed a BPS-accredited conversion qualification and have a BPS-approved postgraduate qualification and training to doctoral level, will be able to become chartered members of the coaching psychology division (BPS 2021b). The requisites are explicit and, as is the case for instance, with clinical psychology or counselling psychology, coaching psychology will now be a recognized profession. It will be interesting to see if this change causes significant rumblings in other countries where coaching psychology is well established, such as Australia.

The practice of psychology in coaching psychology

Psychologists, through their training and mandated regular supervision of practice, become scientists – practitioners, or as Iordanou et al. (2017) have more recently suggested, scholar-practitioners. The reflective space of their training, supervision and critical reflection aids their development as people, as practitioners and as coaches (Hawkins et al. 2019, 2021). Their understanding of what, why and when they do what they do provides them with the capacity to critically reflect on the science of human behaviour, to understand and make contextually appropriate judgements and provide answers: that is, to practise ethically (Biswas-Diener and van Nieuwerburgh 2021).

The practice of a coaching psychologist is informed by various fields of study, such as developmental psychology, personality, learning and training, psychometrics, and often positive psychology and clinical psychology (Palmer and Whybrow 2007b). Global surveys have been undertaken to capture how coaching psychologists view their role and the 'how' of their practice. The findings were significant in that coaching psychologists describe their 'how' as primarily facilitation with the addition of some instruction, but that this works across a dimension rather than in a silo of one way of being (see Palmer and Whybrow 2007a, 2019, for a full review). The surveys also captured the theories and approaches coaching psychologists use in their practice, and found a vast range of psychological-based coaching, such as solution-focused, cognitive behavioural, positive psychology and some integrative approaches (Palmer and Whybrow 2019).

With the regulation of coaching psychology comes the obligations of practice: namely, the need to remain abreast of current research in psychology and coaching, to undertake professional development, and to take part in supervision by either a psychologist or a coaching psychologist, accounting for this through record-keeping and reflection. The requirements are determined by the bodies overseeing psychologist registration (for example, the BPS).

Anthony Grant (2016) has proposed that evidence-based coaching is an amalgamation and synthesis of various life experiences, the wisdom of those experiences, the science of coaching and behaviour change into coaching practice (see Figure 3.1 for an overview of these domains). We suggest the various domains in Figure 3.1 are also influenced by and influence the systems with which they are connected.

We also consider that coaching psychologists are well placed to provide a unique contribution to coaching: the dual focus of solution-focused, goal orientation and a key understanding of human motivation and change important in the facilitation of the well-being and development of a coachee, whether that be

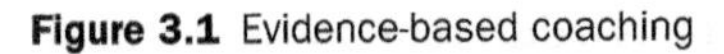
Figure 3.1 Evidence-based coaching

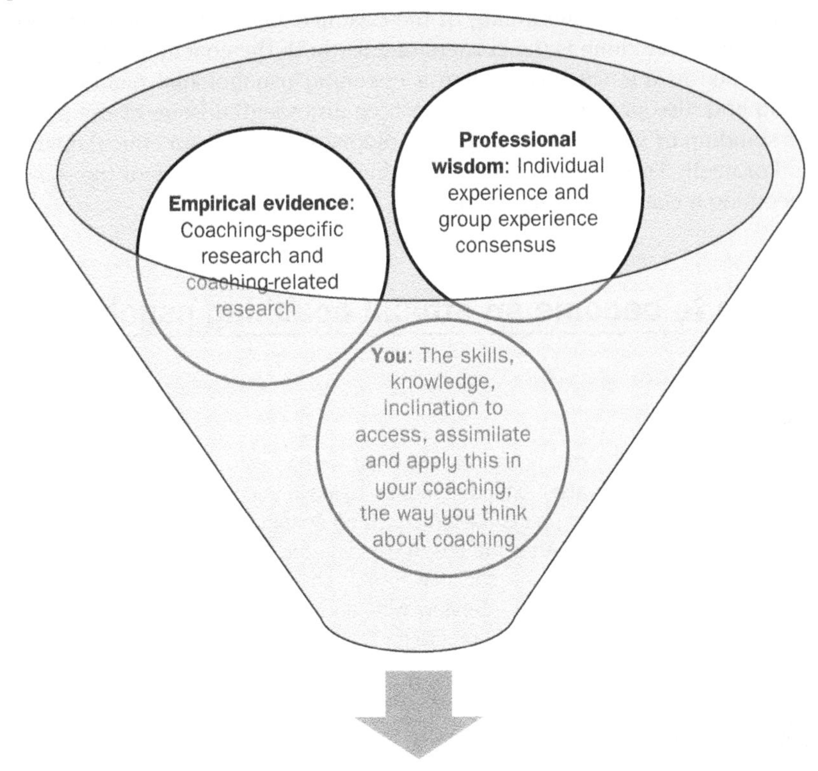

for the individual (Atad et al. 2021), or the team and their interweaving complex systems (Clutterbuck 2021).

Ethics for the coaching psychologist

Ethics are moral principles, laden with one's values, beliefs and knowledge. Ethical guidelines for a coaching psychologist are a fundamental component of coaching practice for accreditability, and are legal obligations if they are also a psychologist. The concern is that a coaching psychologist must remain aware of when they are moving into a clinical or counselling scenario and undertake decision-making processes to identify this and decide whether they are working within the area(s) of their training and competency (Cavanagh and Buckley 2014; Giraldez-Hayes 2021). However, a tension still exists as to 'who' or 'what' coaches coach: do they coach clinical and non-clinical populations? Lai (2014: 75) suggests coaching psychology 'aims to help or facilitate non-clinical populations for sustained behavioural changes through psychological evidence-based interventions and process', while work with clinical populations focuses more on identifying and treating mental ill-health and has a different power dynamic due to the increased vulnerability of the coachee. One can argue contracting for the work to be done is the cornerstone for both the coaching psychologist and coachee in this scenario. When a coaching psychologist has additional training and also provides therapy, we face an essential issue of the public's understanding of what a coaching psychologist provides – an ethical dilemma in and of itself. Training and supervision in ethical practice are of the essence in becoming a coaching psychologist.

Training to become an ethical coaching psychologist

Case study

Maria (not the client's real name) is a married woman with young children. She plans to return to work after extended maternity leave and wants help to adapt to the change. Her company pays for ten coaching sessions as part of a women's back-to-work programme. After the coach explains the confidentiality of the sessions and Maria confirms she can talk freely, she shares that she has been headhunted and invited to an interview with another company. Therefore, she would like to use the sessions to prepare for the interview and the possible move.

Dilemma questions

1. What are the ethical considerations for the coaching psychologist?
2. How do we respond when the interests of the client do not coincide with those of the company that pays for the coaching?
3. How does the coaching psychologist handle their responsibility with the client and the organization in terms of confidentiality?
4. Should the coaching psychologist disclose this to the company? Why yes and why not?

As professionals, coaching psychologists make decisions regularly. Some are about who and how they will serve, others about boundaries, dual relationships, confidentiality or conflicts of interest, to mention just a few. As in Maria's example, these and other issues present ethical dilemmas: 'decision-making problems between two possible moral imperatives, neither of which is unambiguously acceptable or preferable' (IOMC, n.d.). In fact, there are always different options for resolving an ethical dilemma, and some might feel right, but also complex and uncomfortable. In general, solving an ethical dilemma is a complex process requiring knowledge, skills and practice. The question is when and how do coaches develop these skills and engage in the training that will help them deal with ethical issues? Let us try to find some answers.

Ethical decision-making in coaching psychology is more than reflecting when confronted with a good practice issue or a specific dilemma. Just as becoming an excellent coaching psychologist requires training and experience, becoming an ethical coaching psychologist demands both training and experience. Different elements play a part in developing an ethical coaching psychologist, including ethics education, trainees' traits, moral reflection and developing a professional ethical identity.

Ethics education

Coaching psychology ethics competency is a crucial component of the profession, and ethics education should be a significant element of coaches' training. When considering training in the ethical practice of coaching psychology, the issue should be pondered at least from two perspectives: who is teaching, and the what and how of teaching.

Trainers' ethical expertise is essential to face the profession's challenges and prepare students for ethical practice. Research in psychology (Rosenberg and Heimberg 2009; Rowe-Johnson 2018) suggests that trainers are often role models for professional conduct. Therefore, coaching psychology trainers should be aware of the principal ethical codes of practice and model a specific way of being (Rogers 1995), including robust character traits such as honesty, competence, fairness, responsibility, integrity and respect. Assuming that trainers are prepared to model ethical behaviours, the question is what and how to teach ethical practices in coaching psychology.

One of the most obvious considerations is that trainers should help students to become familiar with the main codes of ethics, that is 'a set of ethical principles regulating the conduct of the professional towards the ... client, transcending his own moral, religious or political views and applying throughout the whole range of professional practice' (Havard 1985: 8).

However, we should not think that becoming familiar with the codes of ethics is enough. Codes can be fuzzy and only offer straightforward solutions for complex and ambiguous problems. Without a doubt, they are good guides. Nevertheless, training must be an opportunity to explore critical questions such as what it means to be a coaching psychologist, or what is good or bad, moral or immoral, right or wrong when dealing with specific ethical dilemmas. Such a philosophical approach is essential to understanding ethics and interpreting the application of the different ethics codes' guidance. That could be undertaken by inviting students to engage in ethical dilemmas, discussions and role-play activities – for example, presenting challenging situations and difficult conversations, or sharing case studies for trainees to develop the ability to make ethical choices and identify unethical behaviours and actions. In terms of methodology, the APPEAR model (Passmore and Turner 2018; Passmore and Sinclair 2020) is useful to guide trainees' thinking and improve their decision-making. The model provides a phased process, with six non-linear stages that go from creating ethical awareness to recognizing the consequences of making ethical choices: Awareness, Practice, Possibilities, Extending the field, Acting on reflections, and Reflecting on learning.

Of particular interest for this chapter is also the Guidance on Teaching and Assessment of Ethical Competence in Psychology Education, as it offers 'a framework for good practice in the teaching and assessment of ethical competence in psychology education' (BPS 2015). The framework is based on a four-component model suggested by Rest (1982): ethical sensitivity – to interpret the situation and identify the ethical issue; reasoning – to consider possible approaches based on moral reasoning and to identify the ethical ideal solution; motivation – to decide what to do; and implementation – to implement the identified moral or ethical ideal.

Trainees' personal traits

Students have different personal traits, including their moral values and beliefs. One of the purposes of training is to help them review those traits in the light of ethical principles and rules that may or may not be congruent with their own. Coaching psychology training should not fail to notice these personal traits and the role they play in the individual's professional development, as they will always impact the trainee's perspectives on ethics (Handelsman et al. 2005).

Moral reasoning and reflection

Coaching psychology training must encourage moral reasoning and reflection for students to become morally aware, understand their values in specific situations, take perspective, discern between right and wrong, and develop self-knowledge and self-criticism skills to make thoughtful ethical decisions (Carroll and Shaw 2013). Case studies and supervision provide unique opportunities to engage in one-to-one or group moral reasoning and reflection.

Developing a professional ethical identity

Professional ethical identity results from the integration of the individual's personal and professional world views and values (Gibson et al. 2010). The path of developing professional ethical identity in coaching psychology goes beyond awareness and knowledge of the codes of ethics. It demands the responsibility of continuous ethics education and supervision to fully understand and value the philosophical rational and moral virtues that underpin coaching psychology ethical standards.

Ethical codes and issues in coaching practice

Codes of ethics in different professional bodies

Best practice is a concept that is used to help, guide and protect the coachee and coach, whether they are a coach or coaching psychologist. In the realm of coaching, a plethora of ethical guidelines are available to help guide coaches' ethical thinking and practice. The leading professional bodies, including the ICF (International Coaching Federation), the EMCC (European Mentoring and Coaching Council), the Association for Coaching, the WBECS (World Business and Executive Coach Summit) or the International Organization for Business Coaching, are signatories of an overarching ethical framework, the Global Code of Ethics (2021) for coaching, mentoring and supervision, jointly created in 2016 by EMCC and the Association for Coaching. Coaching psychologists, however, are registered psychologists, which in many countries is a protected title, and so abide by or follow the code of ethics framed within the territory where they are registered. For example, the British Psychological Society provides essential guidelines and policy directives in several documents, including the BPS Code of Ethics and Conduct (BPS 2018), the BPS Practice Guidelines (2017) and the BPS Code of Human Research Ethics (2021a).

Practising coaching psychology ethically

Coaching psychologists, if they have completed a comprehensive psychology training, will have integrated ethical considerations such as privacy, duty of care or informed consent into their practice. They will also have integrated ethical decision-making processes into coaching, and understand and use supervision to support their thinking through ethical dilemmas and the considerations and legal boundaries of dual relationships. An example of a dual relationship may be a coach working in a remote area, and so may be faced with having to make a decision as to whether they should coach a friend. Or from a legal standpoint a psychologist, and so a coaching psychologist, is not allowed to engage in a romantic relationship with a coachee. The thinking through how to hold this dual relationship and keep professional boundaries of confidentiality and neutrality in the coaching will need to be continually explored – supervision in this instance is of paramount importance.

Tensions for coaching psychology and ethical codes

A coaching psychologist who is not yet a chartered coaching psychologist, therefore not obliged in practice by a protected title, has options, it would seem, as to which code of ethics they use to help guide their coaching practice. The legalities are not clear. If a psychologist is acting as a coach, are they still bound by the protected title and so guided by the code of ethics in the territory they are registered with? Or are they relieved of the legal obligation of the protected title and able to refer to any of the coaching codes of ethics available? See the case study and reflective questions for consideration.

Case study

A coach and a coaching psychologist together created and delivered a public workshop on well-being for parents. During the registration process, a parent, Josie (not her real name), wrote to the coaching psychologist and coach to explain their very difficult circumstances at home.

Josie works as a homemaker and is married to Martin, who works in a bank. They have five children aged 3 to 10 years old. All five have significant psychosocial concerns and some form of learning and behavioural challenges, both at home and at school. Josie feels she is unable to cope most days and would like a rest; she is in need of significant medical, psychiatric and psychological support for both herself, her husband and all five children. She is hoping the workshop will give her some new insights into how she may better cope or try to care for herself.

The coach and coaching psychologist responded to Josie's email, empathizing with her obvious distress, and suggested she speak with the coaching psychologist prior to the workshop. The coaching psychologist wished to assess whether attendance was the best course of action for Josie. It was decided that, if Josie did attend the workshop, she would at the very least receive a couple of hours' respite from the challenges at home. Additionally, Josie had planned to attend with friends, enabling her to socialize and also be in the company of intimate support if needed. Hence it was decided her attendance at the workshop would not do any harm.

The psychologist decided significant intervention was needed at home, and chose to connect Josie to the local special needs professional association, where she would have access to a range of therapeutic interventions.

The coach did not take part in the conversations, however, the coaching psychologist did provide the coach with an overview so they were aware in case the coaching psychologist was required to provide Josie with extra support or intervention at any time during the workshop.

Dilemma questions

1. What are the ethical considerations for both the coach and the coaching psychologist?
2. Are the considerations and areas of responsibility different or the same – how and in what way?
3. If they were different – why? What could the implications be for the coach, and for the coaching psychologist?
4. How would you use the APPEAR model to work through the dilemma? What would it look like?

Professional challenges and accountability

Understanding the complexity of the modern world is essential in order to consider coaching psychology professional challenges and accountability. It has been argued that the Covid-19 pandemic accelerated the transition from uncertainty to chaos, from 'VUCA' to 'BANI'. Emerging after the end of the Cold War, the VUCA concept (US Army Heritage and Education Center 2019) describes a volatile, uncertain, complex and ambiguous world in constant change, and its impact on people's and companies' lives. Some years later, the Covid-19 pandemic led to a scenario in which VUCA did not seem enough to describe the new reality. As a result, a new framework, BANI, created by the futurologist Jamais Cascio, emerged. BANI means 'brittle', 'anxiety', 'non-linearity' and 'incomprehensible' (Cascio 2020). In a BANI world, coaching psychologists work with clients living in a world where a catastrophe can happen at any time, and employment and business are more fragile than ever before (brittle). This is a world where anxiety is a prevalent symptom both for individuals and the job market, and life and work events seem disconnected and disproportionate (non-linear). In a world where the answers we receive do not make sense and make us realize there are many things we cannot control (incomprehensible), coaching psychologists have the challenge and the responsibility to ethically find new ways to support clients to adapt and grow. Amid this scenario, several professional issues have ethical implications, including the development of technological systems and AI; equity, equality, diversity and inclusion in coaching or mental health; and the boundaries between coaching and other helping professions. Considering the devastating impact of the pandemic on people's mental health (see, for example, WHO 2020), it is not surprising that more and more coaching psychologists report or bring to supervision topics related to clients' mental health or distress. Therefore, among the challenges for coaching psychologists, this section will refer to mental health issues and boundaries between coaching and other helping professions.

The boundaries between coaching and other helping professions: ethical issues

It has been argued that one of the main differences between coaching and therapy is that the first deals with non-clinical populations, while the second is for people who present with mental health issues or abnormal levels of distress (Grant and Palmer 2002; Grant 2006). However, some studies suggest that between 25 and 50 per cent of life coaching clients meet clinical mental health criteria (Green et al. 2005; Grant 2006). In this context, it is essential that coaching psychologists can recognize mental health issues in their clients and that they are not perceived by their clients as counsellors, psychotherapists or mental health professionals.

As mentioned, psychologists come to the coaching psychology profession from many different backgrounds, e.g. organizational psychology, clinical psychology or sports psychology. Nevertheless, the professional and ethical practice requires coaches to identify and respect the limits of their practice – or, in other words, not to go beyond the boundaries between coaching and other helping professions. To promise solutions to clients with mental health issues, neglecting that they could benefit from other kinds of intervention, is unethical and potentially harmful. In their contract, coaches should clarify that coaching is not a substitute for counselling or psychotherapy, and they are not trained to offer diagnosis, treatment or therapy. Oddly enough, the coaching codes of ethics do not refer to the boundaries between coaching and therapy. Only the ICF (2021) has released a set of evidence-based resources for referring clients to therapy.

Although coaching psychologists should know when a client needs to be referred to psychotherapy or another specialized intervention, referring a client entails an ethical dilemma that should be addressed individually or in supervision. Let us imagine you were the coach for the client described in the following case study. What would have been your decision and course of action?

Case study

Maxwell Smith (not his real name) was a senior sales manager at a pharmaceutical company. According to HR, Maxwell had experienced some problems with his team members. However, because he was an excellent salesman, HR had always tried to sort out the difficulties. Nevertheless, the situation reached breaking point when Maxwell shouted and publicly humiliated one of his employees during a team meeting. After that incident, HR decided to assign a coach to Maxwell, to set goals to improve the relationships with some members of the team. Soon after the coaching process started, the coach realized that Maxwell had a narcissistic personality disorder, and that was the cause of his lack of empathy and troubled relationships. Coaching could only have worked as a sticking plaster to stem the bleeding from a deep wound, as a narcissistic personality disorder requires special psychological treatment. How does a coaching psychologist come to this conclusion? What is the right course of action? What are the ethical decisions and actions in this case?

Dilemma questions

1 What is the best course of action in this case?
2 Should the coach continue working with the client? Why yes, and why not? What would be the impact either way?
3 How could the APPEAR model help the coaching psychologist to work through this dilemma?
4 How does the coaching psychologist handle a referral?

Conclusion

Coaching and coaching psychology, while appearing very similar, have different responsibilities and accountabilities when clients present with significant ethical concerns. Both are unregulated professions globally, though in recent times the BPS has gained acceptance for the inclusion of the title Chartered Coaching Psychologist. However, this chartership only serves the United Kingdom.

Other countries, such as Australia, France and the United States, protect the use of the title 'psychologist' alone. This point in itself poses many problems for a global regulation and ethical code of practice for coaching, which some would like to see.

Mature and ethical coaching practice must be driven by a set of strong ethical principles, and must follow ethical guidelines in delivering the practice. Coaching psychology is a relatively new discipline but is heavily influenced by its umbrella profession psychology in theory, and training in ethical practice. Coaching psychology, although an unregulated profession, finds its accountability and integrity in practice through various coaching bodies' ethical codes, including psychology ethical guidelines.

The challenges in discerning the boundaries of the practice of coaching by non-psychologists and those who use the title of coaching psychologist in the regions where the title is unregulated are an unresolved conundrum. Supervision by suitably experienced and psychologically minded supervisors can be argued to be a crucial factor for all coaches. An understanding of ethical decision-making is key to maintaining responsible coaching practice.

References

Atad, O., Smith, W.A. and Green, S. (2021) Coaching as the missing ingredient in the application and training of positive psychological science, in W.A. Smith, I. Boniwell and S. Green (eds) *Positive Psychology Coaching in the Workplace*. Cham: Springer, pp. 41–60.

Biswas-Diener, R. and van Nieuwerburgh, C. (2021) The professionalization of positive psychology coaching, in W.A. Smith, I. Boniwell and S. Green (eds) *Positive Psychology Coaching in the Workplace*. Cham: Springer, pp. 23–40.

BPS (British Psychological Society) (2015) *Guidance on Teaching and Assessment of Ethical Competence in Psychology Education*, BPS website. Available at: https://www.bps.org.uk/news-and-policy/guidance-teaching-and-assessment-ethical-competence-psychology-education-2015 (accessed 16 May 2022).

BPS (British Psychological Society) (2017) *BPS Practice Guidelines (2017)*, BPS website. Available at: https://www.bps.org.uk/news-and-policy/practice-guidelines (accessed 16 May 2022).

BPS (British Psychological Society) (2018) *Code of Ethics and Conduct*, BPS website. Available at: https://www.bps.org.uk/news-and-policy/bps-code-ethics-and-conduct (accessed 16 May 2022).

BPS (British Psychological Society) (2021a) *BPS Code of Human Research Ethics*, BPS website. Available at: https://www.bps.org.uk/news-and-policy/bps-code-human-research-ethics (accessed 16 May 2022).

BPS (British Psychological Society) (2021b) *Standards for the Accreditation of Coaching Psychology Programmes*. Leicester: The British Psychological Society Partnership and Accreditation. Available at: https://www.bps.org.uk/sites/www.bps.org.uk/files/Accreditation/Standards%20for%20the%20accreditation%20of%20Coaching%20Psychology%20programmes.pdf (accessed 16 May 2022).

Carroll, M. and Shaw, E. (2013) *Ethical Maturity in the Helping Professions: Making Difficult Life and Work Decisions*. London: Jessica Kingsley Publishers.

Cascio, J. (2020) Facing the Age of Chaos, Medium website. Available at: https://medium.com/@cascio/facing-the-age-of-chaos-b00687b1f51d (accessed 16 May 2022).

Cavanagh, M. and Buckley, A. (2014) Coaching and mental health, in E. Cox, T. Bachkirova and D. Clutterbuck (eds) *The Complete Handbook of Coaching*, 2nd edn. London: Sage, pp. 405–17.

Clutterbuck, D. (2021) Coaching teams positively from a complex, adaptive systems perspective, in W.A. Smith, I. Boniwell and S. Green (eds) *Positive Psychology Coaching in the Workplace*. Cham: Springer, pp. 297–316.

Gibson, D.M., Dollarhide, C.T. and Moss, J.M. (2010) Professional identity development: A grounded theory of transformational tasks of new counsellors, *Counselor Education and Supervision*, 50(1): 21–38.

Giraldez-Hayes, A. (2021) Different domains or grey areas? Setting boundaries between coaching and therapy: A thematic analysis, *The Coaching Psychologist*, 17(2): 18–29.

Global Code of Ethics (2021) *Global Code of Ethics for Coaches, Mentors, and Supervisors*. Available at: https://emccuk.org/Common/Uploaded%20files/Policies/Global_Code_of_Ethics_EN_v3.pdf (accessed 16 May 2022).

Grant, A.M. (2006) A personal perspective on professional coaching and the development of coaching psychology, *International Coaching Psychology Review*, 1(1): 12–22.

Grant, A.M. (2008) Past, present and future: The evolution of professional coaching and coaching psychology, in S. Palmer and A. Whybrow (eds) *Handbook of Coaching Psychology: A Guide* for *Practitioners*. New York: Routledge, pp. 23–39.

Grant, A.M. (2016) What constitutes evidence-based coaching?: A two-by-two framework for distinguishing strong from weak evidence for coaching, *International Journal of Evidence Based Coaching and Mentoring*, 14(1): 74–85.

Grant, A. and Palmer, S. (2002) Coaching psychology. Workshop and meeting held at the Annual Conference of the Division of Counselling Psychology, British Psychological Society, Torquay, 18 May.

Green, S., Oades, L. and Grant, A. (2005) An evaluation of a life-coaching group programme: Initial findings from a waitlist control study, in M. Cavanagh, A. Grant and T. Kemps (eds) *Evidence-Based Coaching*, Vol. 1: *Theory, Research and Practice from the Behavioural Science*. Queensland: Australian Academic Press, pp. 127–42.

Handelsman, M.M., Gottlieb, M.C. and Knapp, S. (2005) Training ethical psychologists: An acculturation model, *Professional Psychology: Research and Practice*, 36(1): 59–65.

Hawkins, P., Allan, J. and Turner, E. (2021) Supervision: Widening the lens and perspective – the art of reflective practice, in W.A. Smith, I. Boniwell and S. Green (eds) *Positive Psychology Coaching in the Workplace*. Cham: Springer, pp. 141–55.

Hawkins, P., Turner, E. and Passmore, J. (2019) *The Manifesto for Coaching Supervision*. Henley-on-Thames: Association for Coaching, and Henley Business School. Available at: https://www.henley.ac.uk/news/2019/the-manifesto-for-coaching-supervision (accessed 16 May 2022).

Havard, J. (1985) Medical confidence, *Journal of Medical Ethics*, 11(1): 8–11.

ICF (International Coach Federation) (2021) ICF releases resources for referring clients to therapy, ICF website. Available at: https://coachingfederation.org/blog/icf-releases-resources-for-referring-clients-to-therapy (accessed 16 May 2022).

IOMC (International Online Medical Council) (n.d.) *Ethical-Dilemma Peer-Review Journals*, IOMC website. Available at: https://www.iomcworld.org/medical-journals/ethical-dilemma-peerreview-journals-37941.html (accessed 16 May 2022).

Iordanou, I., Hawley, R. and Iordanou, C. (2017) *Values and Ethics in Coaching*. London: Sage.

Lai, Y. L. (2014) Enhancing evidence-based coaching through the development of a coaching psychology competency framework: Focus on the coaching relationship. PhD thesis, University of Surrey. Available at: https://www.proquest.com/openview/43a1e125b49e55fb34fa32dad427b020/1?pq-origsite=gscholar&cbl=51922&diss=y (accessed 16 May 2022).

Palmer, S. and Whybrow, A. (eds) (2007a) *Handbook of Coaching Psychology: A Guide for Practitioners*. New York: Routledge.

Palmer, S. and Whybrow, A. (2007b) Past, present and future, in S. Palmer and A. Whybrow (eds) *Handbook of Coaching Psychology: A Guide for Practitioners*. New York: Routledge.

Palmer, S. and Whybrow, A. (eds) (2019) *Handbook of Coaching Psychology: A Guide for Practitioners*, 2nd edn. New York: Routledge.

Passmore, J. (ed.) (2021) *The Coaches' Handbook: The Complete Practitioner Guide for Professional Coaches*. New York: Routledge.

Passmore, J. and Lai, Y.-L. (2019) Coaching psychology: Exploring definitions and research contribution to practice?, *International Coaching Psychology Review*, 14(2): 69–83.

Passmore, J. and Sinclair, T. (2020) *Becoming a Coach: The Essential ICF Guide*. Cham: Springer.

Passmore, J. and Turner, E. (2018) Reflections on integrity: The APPEAR model, *Coaching at Work*, 13(2): 42–6.

Rest, J.R. (1982) A psychologist looks at the teaching of ethics, *The Hastings Center Report*, 12(1): 29–36.

Rogers, C.R. (1995) *A Way of Being*. Boston, MA: Houghton Mifflin Harcourt.

Rosenberg A. and Heimberg R.G. (2009) Ethical issues in mentoring doctoral students in clinical psychology, *Cognitive and Behavioral Practice*, 16(2): 181–90.

Rowe-Johnson, M. (2018) Achieving ethical mentoring and mentee professional integrity through formal mentor training for practicing psychologists, *Training and Education in Professional Psychology*, 12(3): 203–9. https://doi.org/10.1037/tep0000198

US Army Heritage & Education Center (2019) Who first originated the term VUCA (Volatility, Uncertainty, Complexity and Ambiguity)? USAHEC Ask Us a Question (website). Available at: https://usawc.libanswers.com/faq/84869 (accessed 16 May 2022).

WHO (World Health Organization) (2020) Covid-19 disrupting mental health services in most countries, WHO Survey. WHO. Available at: https://www.who.int/news/item/05-10-2020-covid-19-disrupting-mental-health-services-in-most-countries-who-survey (accessed 16 May 2022).

A coaching practitioner's model: The selective realism conceptual model

Manfusa Shams

Summary

The progress of coaching psychology practice needs to be supported by an appropriate theoretical model. Theorizing coaching psychology effectively can provide strong groundwork for the successful delivery of coaching practice. Due to the increasing practical value of coaching psychology, it is important to develop theoretical knowledge encompassing coaching practice, and relevant practice-focused models to support the delivery effectively.

This chapter offers a new coaching psychology practitioner model using the 'selective realism' concept. This promising new concept has provided emphasis on the fully functional capabilities of individuals to achieve their maximum potential, which can be nurtured and developed, changed and advanced using selective realism during the coaching intervention. The model has been developed for practitioners to apply to their practice, with a focus on the need for theorizing coaching practice to develop, deliver and maintain good ethical practice. The selective realism conceptual model offers a practical model for practitioners and, as such, it has strong potential to become a key guide and a companion reference point for coaching psychology practitioners.

Keywords: selective realism, coaching psychology practice, practitioners' model, psychology paradigm, holism, multiple processors.

Introduction

Coaching psychology is still not recognized as a distinctive practice-based scientific discipline around the world. The slow progress in rolling out coaching psychology and coaching psychology practice to every corner of the world is due to the lack of evidence-based research, theories and models specific to coaching psychology, poor communication and dissemination of value-based coaching practice using psychological knowledge and principles, and a lack of publicity and publications.

The advancement of coaching psychology is also affected by the conflicting usage of the term 'coaching psychologist' vs 'coach'. The latter term is used generally all over the world to represent a training specialist who guides and instructs individuals how to learn new skills and techniques to perform according to an accepted standard. This is a directive approach in which the individuals under a coach's training programme have limited autonomy to guide their own behaviour. A coach in this context is mainly delivering a prescribed formula for learning to achieve the required standard for goal attainment, e.g. football training, athletics training, acting, etc. Coaching psychology is, however, the opposite end of the spectrum of this popular meaning of the term coach (Figure 4.1).

The term coaching attached to coaching psychology is often misinterpreted as a type of training discipline, as the emphasis is put on the term 'coach' rather than psychology. Chapter 1 and Chapter 2 have presented the discussion on the dominant influence of psychology in coaching practice, and confirmed that coaching psychology is not a training-focused discipline but a scientific practice-based discipline to support an individual's growth and development using psychological principles, knowledge and evidence.

It is essential for coaching psychologists and coaching psychologist practitioners to develop strong, distinctive theoretical models and an evidence-based framework to enhance and maintain good practice in coaching psychology. This will not only help to gain recognition as a unique scientific discipline and a psychology-driven professional practice, but is also expected to educate the general public in all societies about this emerging scientific discipline, which is not related to the popular term 'coach' or 'guided training'.

Figure 4.1 Distinctive differences between coaching psychology and coaching practice

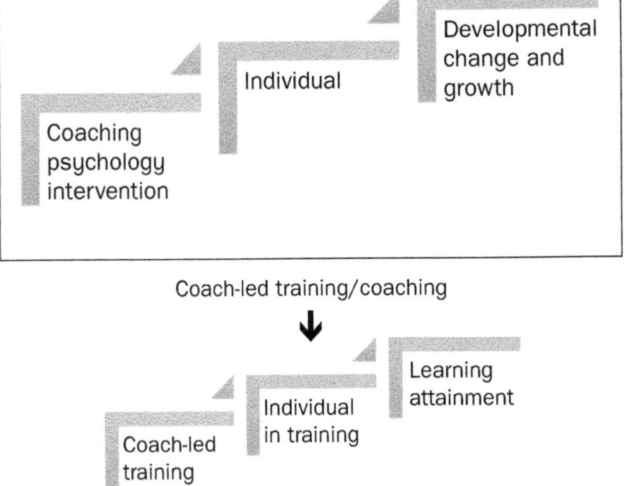

Aims

The aim of this chapter is to present a conceptual model of 'selective realism' for coaching practitioners. Selective realism refers to enabling understanding and awareness of self in the light of one's present life experiences to make selective changes in behaviour for the optimum level of performance and achievement.

The rationale of this model is to offer a new paradigm for coaching psychology to understand individuals' developmental progress in a coaching context, to apply the model to coaching practice, and to support developing individuals using 'selective realism', which is grounded on a 'holistic approach'. Environment is strongly embedded in human development, hence an enriched environment can ensure the effective functions of all major systems (neurological, cognitive and behavioural) in an individual seeking coaching intervention. The model aims to highlight the impact of the environment on self-selected realization as determined by sensory processors, knowledge and life experiences.

The key feature of this conceptual model is the enabling and personal agency of individuals to reinterpret their life experiences, and to provide directive meanings towards changes of a holistic self (neurological, cognitive and behavioural).

The selective realism conceptual model

It is important to understand the critical roles of selected sensory and behavioural elements in a coaching intervention. The selection of these elements by a coachee depends on the extent to which they are able to interpret and reconstruct their present life conditions in order to facilitate changes in behaviour and cognition, and to enhance and maintain a fully functional self. A coaching intervention helps a coachee to achieve this transformational change to attain their full potential during the coaching sessions, which is also expected to be sustained after the end of the coaching sessions.

A change in environment is needed for individuals to enable their selective realism for behavioural optimization. Changing the environment refers to changes in the existing environment in which an individual is living and working, and interacting with others. Individuals have the capabilities to recreate and relive their experiences, and to refine their selection of sensory, feelings and behavioural responses to the environment. The environment in a coaching context refers to the present coaching environment, and coaching sessions may serve as stimuli for the individual to achieve 'selective realism'.

In this practitioners' model, I have highlighted the underlying psychological properties of coaching practice that can provide an inclusive developmental approach to individuals seeking coaching intervention. This includes neurological, behavioural and cognitive elements impacting on individuals' development and performance simultaneously (Figure 4.2). These elements are regulated by the environmental change factors.

Figure 4.2 A selective realism conceptual coaching practitioner model

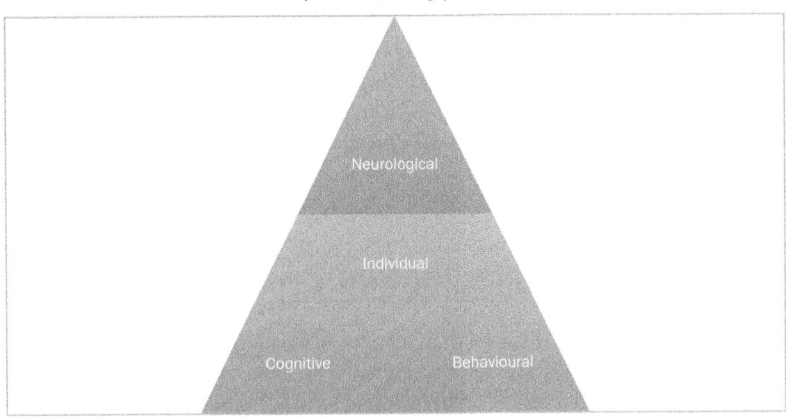

The functions of these multiple elements are regulated by selective realism. Selective realism guides an individual to be proactive to achieve an expected behavioural outcome in relation to a changing environment.

The dominant environmental change factor is the change in the social setting of the coachee – e.g. leadership coaching must consider the environmental changes of the leader to execute their functions, and this could be changing from an authoritarian to an egalitarian work environment. This proposed concept (selective realism) has a developmental characteristic, and this relates to a new way of thinking, feeling and behaving using the learning and experiences from the coaching sessions. The neurological and cognitive elements provide a collective influence on the forward-looking behavioural performance.

From an educational perspective, a coaching intervention aided by an inclusive developmental approach generates selective realism, which can influence the performance of the learners as it takes into account cognitive and behavioural elements in learning. The neurological progression is embedded in the developmental change, and can be traced, measured and identified using relevant tools and techniques.

The selective realism concept offers a new paradigm of understanding coaching psychology in practice. Unlike the existing singular theoretical approach in which coaching interventions are predominantly focused on the underlying psychological factors in behavioural change, the selective realism conceptual model emphasizes the self as comprised of present relived experiences, maintained, regulated, and advanced by neuro-cognitive-behavioural elements of the individual. The inclusive approach proposed in this model has not yet been explored, although the value of coaching psychology practice is increasingly recognized and included in many different practices, such as education, health and sports.

An inclusive and integrated multi-agency intervention to support individuals' development can be achieved from the application of this model. It also has a forward-looking approach to follow up the developmental stages, and to reinforce the changes using subsequent coaching interventions. The inclusive and integrated approach is grounded on the notion of a 'holistic' approach in which all key developmental elements are intrinsically intertwined to facilitate expected changes in individuals' behavioural, cognitive and neurological functions. The wraparound environmental change factors are the supportive agents to achieve selective realism.

Environmental change factors

Environmental changes refer to the perceived changes in personal agency of an individual in the coaching environment. The transformational change can provide a powerful, sustained positive outcome for the individual. For example, a task-focused leader may overlook the good relationship building needs of the team, as such team building was never recognized as an important part of the leader's role. A leader can recognize this shortfall in their leadership and the working environment may change as a result of this coaching intervention.

The influence of coaching context has been researched extensively (Shams 2011; Martin et al. 2014; Greif and Benning-Rohnke 2015). However, intentional change in the environment has not been researched explicitly in a coaching context. The environmental change is usually expected to occur after the coaching intervention; for example, role change in a business environment is linked to a different office environment, or changing dietary practice may lead to a different lifestyle through health coaching. Intentional change here refers to changing the environment during the coaching intervention to assess the effect on the individual's performance, and to compare this with the quality and level of performance at pre-coaching level to confirm the positive influence of a coaching intervention. This may help to identify if the coaching environment has a negative impact on reaching the peak performance level independent of the influence of other psychological factors. Selective realism provides a new approach to apply to generate psychological space or a personalized environment for the individual to thrive naturally.

Individuals are susceptible to changes in the environment, and this relates to changing beliefs, attitudes and personality (Hughes 2002; McCrae and Costa 2003; Martin et al. 2014). A coaching psychology practice is designed to support the required internal and external changing needs of a coachee – e.g. changes in belief will lead to changes in behaviour. The intentional change theory proposed by Boyatzis (2006) on individuals' capability to change did not highlight the importance of environmental change in sustaining behavioural change. Intentional change theory supports the changes in the neuronal pathway through practice and mastery. The emphasis is on cognition.

One of the major cautions is that some individuals are resistant to change. The change process can be supported by helping motivation to change in terms of helping the individual to recognize the benefits of change, and how to manage change (Rollnick et al. 1999). Increasing intrinsic motivation helps coachees to change through psychological stimulation and arousal (Boyatzis and Akrivou 2006). An appropriate coaching intervention can provide this psychological stimulation and arousal for the coachee. There have been discussions on the length of coaching sessions required for making effective sustainable changes, e.g. ten coaching sessions (Green et al. 2007; Martin et al. 2014). I am proposing that there should not be any limitations or boundary imposed on coaching sessions as this should be tailored to the needs of individuals to address diversity and complexity in coaching needs. The environmental change factors in the selective realism conceptual model therefore are not time-bound or culturally specific. This environmentally friendly-driven model has the potential to achieve the universal recognition to apply to a coaching practice, with the aim of supporting an individual's holistic development. Coaching intervention provides a logical context to bring changes in an individual's behaviour (Martin et al. 2012), hence coaching practitioners are in a privileged position to facilitate both the changes in individuals and in their immediate environment. Coaching is a co-creative endeavour in which a coach facilitates changes in the thinking, feeling and actions of a coachee through verbal and non-verbal communication. This word 'co-creation' resonates with the famous slogan, 'together we can make it' (Greif and Benning-Rohnke 2015).

The new paradigm in coaching proposed here focuses on the active agency of the individual, which in interaction with their present environment brings changes in neurological, cognitive and behavioural functions. It represents *realization* of the need for an action in the light of present experience, and to execute the action to achieve the desired outcome.

Coaching psychology practice is not restricted to the supportive role for making changes in behavioural and cognitive functions, but also serves as an active environmental agent facilitating the change and improvement. The following example indicates how an active individual agency is guided by the active environmental agents in the coaching intervention.

An example

A senior administrative manager has been working for a local sports centre for over two years. He is seeking leadership coaching as his performance appraisal demands improvement in his leadership. An initial assessment of his role has obtained various environmental constraint factors, such as overtime work, poor communication with his team due to the high level of absenteeism, lack of support from senior management, and health hazards in the office building (lack of ventilation and natural light, poor technological facilities). The coach must recommend these factors be removed before delivering the coaching intervention, because of the need to establish whether they are affecting his performance. These environmental factors need to be taken into account in the coaching delivery. The criticism in this approach is that a coaching intervention can reveal the negative impact of these environmental influences during the coaching sessions. However, the argument in favour of this approach is that the presence of these environmental factors needs to be included to develop the most appropriate coaching intervention. Furthermore, this will allow the endorsement of a holistic approach in coaching in which environmental factors are accompanied by other psychological factors to support changes and improvement in the individual's performance. A coachee will be able to renew their energy to recapture their personal agency to understand the environmental constraints preventing them gaining the maximum level of performance if the coaching sessions are developed to generate selective realism, and pay attention to the existing environmental constraint factors.

Environmental factors are recognized as essential determinants in achieving successful learning outcomes. A coaching practice is itself a learning process for the coachee and the coach (Shams 2022). Hence, environmental factors must be included in a coaching intervention to provide holistic developmental support to an individual.

A holistic approach in the selective realism conceptual coaching model

There is an ongoing debate on the holistic approach vs the humanistic approach in coaching practice. However, there is no sharp dividing line between these two approaches: rather, a common key construct is used in each approach to understand human behaviour. The common construct prevalent in holistic and humanistic approaches is the 'integrated virtues and values', which operate as a driving force for the development of an individual. A coaching intervention is based on the value-based needs of an individual striving for self-actualization, as offered in Maslow's needs hierarchy model (Gregory and Levy 2012). The humanistic approach is essentially holistic, with a single vision to consider an individual's totality rather than discrete functional elements. The focus is on the integrated functional capabilities of individuals. The meeting point of humanistic and holistic approaches is this 'whole/total functional individual' with the capability to change, develop, grow and make sustained progress (Cassidy 2010). The adaptation capability is inherently built within the whole functional individual in relation to the challenging environment.

The proposed selective realism conceptual model emphasizes the interconnected multiple functioning elements of an individual which respond to a coaching intervention simultaneously, thus enabling understanding and realization of selected life experiences to lead to further change and development. A coaching intervention needs to support the multilayered developmental changes to ensure that each layer is interacting with the others effectively, and to explore the level of interactions to achieve the desired changes and coaching outcomes.

If the level and extent of changes in the three functional areas (neurological, cognitive and behavioural) can be traced using relevant approaches and

Figure 4.3 The impact of selective realism on three main systems (neurological, cognitive, behavioural)

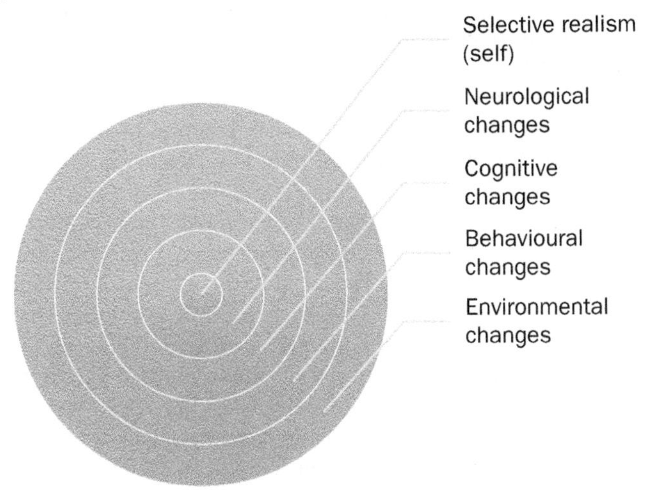

techniques, then a coaching intervention will be effective in achieving the expected sustained outcome. This will lead to a growing critical mass of coaching psychology knowledge and raise the scientific status of coaching psychology as an evidence-based discipline. Figure 4.3 depicts the areas of change during coaching intervention. The multilayered developmental changes are caused by three major systems, as described in the following sections.

Neurological element

In Chapter 1, we discussed the need to trace the neurological basis of coaching interventions in order to make progress in understanding the effects of coaching on the brain functions and cognitive processes (Shams 2015). There has been increasing attention paid to tracing neurological changes in relation to both cognitive and behavioural changes during and after coaching interventions (Riddell 2018). If we can trace the changes in brain functions, then this will also validate the concept of 'neuroplasticity', and brain region function-specificity (Grant 2015). This can be accomplished using neuroscientific tools such as fMRI, which will further strengthen the bond between coaching psychology and neuroscience (Campion 2011). Grant (2015) has asserted that this holistic approach has immense value in coaching psychology practice. The interdisciplinary approach has the potential to challenge the reductionist approach in coaching practice. The reductionist approach is speculative, as it relies on the assumption of changes in brain activities (Grant 2015). Hence, we need a systematic, holistic, interdisciplinary approach to provide a strong foundation for effective evidence-based coaching psychology practice, with the aim of advancing both neuroscience and coaching psychology to meet the challenges of increasing complexity in human behaviour.

Cognitive element

There is now evidence-based support for the influence of cognitive coaching / cognitive behavioural coaching in changing the cognitive functioning of a coachee (Schwartz et al. 2019).

The cognitive element in coaching intervention is a strong indicator of behavioural changes to bring sustained developmental growth. A practitioner can offer the maximum benefits for an individual's sustained development if the behavioural changes caused by cognitive elements are acknowledged and aligned with the neurological changes. For example, the cognitive changes in coaching intervention can reduce cognitive decline through changing health behaviours (Schwartz et al. 2019). The advantage of cognitive coaching/cognitive behavioural coaching is that it is built on a triage support system in which individuals' cognitive, behavioural and neurological changes can be supported and enhanced using relevant coaching tools and techniques (Grant et al. 2009; Gyllensten et al. 2010).

A few research studies have confirmed that cognitive coaching helps to reduce cognitive distortions and thinking errors, enhancing cognitive hardiness, and changing difficult emotions (Green et al. 2006, 2007; Grant et al. 2009). These cognitive changes are evident in behaviour and in the brain functions if these are assessed in a coaching intervention. Cognitive functions are activated during coaching interventions and this in turn brings neurological and behavioural changes. Major cognitive functions include thinking and understanding, problem solving and focused attention. These functional elements are powerful drivers for modifying behaviour, accompanied by changes in neurological functions.

The selective realism conceptual model in practice proposes to formalize coaching intervention practice using this triage system to enable personal agency to make changes and progress in the light of present and new or relived experiences.

It may appear that the model is offering an approach similar to the health and social care system's existing multi-agency practice in which multiple agencies work together to support individuals' health and well-being. The main difference between the multi-agency health and social care practice and the selective realism conceptual model in practice is that the latter does not require multiple different services. Instead, the focus is on the fully functional individuals who are capable of interpreting and reflecting on life experiences to make neurological, cognitive and behavioural changes in response to the coaching intervention. The individual in this context is the active agent who manipulates the changes in reaction to the coaching. This is not similar to medical treatments, as the prescribed medicine or treatment is expected to bring about health changes in patients. The patients here are thus the passive recipients of treatment.

The proposed new selective realism concept is expected to help in understanding individuals' holistic development. We need to consider changes in the total functioning systems of an individual, initiated by the individual themselves. This is important to advance coaching psychology practice towards an effective and efficient holistic scientific discipline for individuals' development and growth.

Behavioural element

Coaching psychology practice is essentially an intervention to change behaviour to improve and maintain optimum performance level. Coaching intervention may act as an active environmental agent to bring changes in the total functioning systems. Since the widely cited GROW model was introduced, there is now strong evidence of significant behavioural change as a result of coaching intervention (Grant et al. 2009). This includes improvement in performance level, lifestyles, relationships and educational attainment (Green et al. 2007).

Behavioural elements are multidimensional, and thus have enabling functions to change various behavioural performances in response to specific stimulations generated from the coaching.

Selective realism provides individuals with a mental map to navigate along millions of bite-sized pieces of information to find a selected few to develop personal agency for self-growth and sustainable progress.

An inclusive, functional selective realism conceptual model

The functional capability of a proposed model is similar to a car engine, which functions well when all the parts in the engine are working together to make for smooth driving. An inclusive, functional selective realism may accompany developmental change indicators for neurological, cognitive and behavioural domains. These change indicators then provide deep insights into the effect of coaching intervention on an individual as a whole, taking account of all major functional parts of the individual. For example, the improved performance of a coachee (behavioural) in their employment context may be the outcome of changing perception of the role-based task (cognitive), with increasing mental capacity (neurological) to accelerate their performance to reach the target in job performance (behavioural). All these changes can be obtained in the coaching outcome measures.

The present coaching practice applies a singular approach with a focus on the behavioural domain only, although the impact on the neurological and cognitive domains is increasingly accepted and acknowledged (Shams 2015). This generates the question of how all major functional parts of an individual are influenced by the coaching intervention. The selective realism conceptual model is an answer to this 'how', as it argues for individuals' own actions in the light of new experiences of understanding self, reflecting on past experiences, and focusing on their present live experience to change and improve their own behaviour.

Application of the selective realism conceptual model

It may appear difficult to implement this new proposed model in coaching psychology practice because of the absence of user-friendly, readily available and cost-effective neurological tools and measures. Although cognitive and behavioural changes during and after the coaching interventions are measured using relevant self-reported psychometric tests and other observational techniques, neurological changes are not yet measured simultaneously. This leads to a caveat in the effectiveness and robustness of coaching psychology practice in comparison with other scientific practice where changes are measured instantly using sophisticated instruments, such as in the medical sciences. Nonetheless, there should be an initiative to develop models and a theoretical paradigm to support the generation of an inclusive developmental model, encompassing a neurological, cognitive and behavioural functional map during and after the coaching interventions, and including active environmental agents affecting individuals' total functioning system.

The selective realism conceptual model aims to provide the essential knowledge base to develop an application tool to implement in coaching practice. Grounded on a holistic approach, this model highlights that individuals, as active agents, interact with their immediate environment to make changes in their neurological, cognitive and behavioural performance. This model provides the scientific warranty for the validity of coaching effects. The formal accreditation of coaching psychology practice must be accompanied by strong theoretical underpinnings of coaching application tools and techniques. The proposed model is expected to be an essential companion of coaching psychology practice, and to meet the needs of appropriate coaching psychology practice applications. A new strand of thought from this model is providing insights into the immense value of an integrated coaching psychology practice, along with theory-driven and evidence-based explanations for changes in the functional systems of an individual attending coaching intervention.

Developing individuals using selective realism

The selective realism concept offers an extended insight in the existing realism of a coachee arising from the coaching sessions. The recurring key issue in coaching psychology research and practice is development and growth. This new concept, selective realism, is grounded on these two fundamental issues: helping individuals: (1) to understand and interpret their live experiences, and (2) to reflect on their thoughts, feelings and actions to bring changes to each of the areas using the support from the coaching sessions. The individuals thus are able to guide their own development, and make maximum efforts to optimize their performance. The model is confirming that the coaching process ensures knowing what is already known to an individual, using new knowledge and learning experiences. Hence, it is not about knowing the unknown self, as

Table 4.1 Emergence of selective realism

In coaching	End of coaching
Neurological changes	Neurological changes
Cognitive changes	Cognitive changes
Behavioural changes	Behavioural changes
Emergence of selective realism	Outcomes of selective realism

obtained in the Johari window framework (Mahoney 2019); rather it is about developing and managing live experiences using a developmental sequence of progression towards self-realization. Self-realization during coaching intervention influences cognitive ability to respond appropriately to the environmental demands. The individuals' sensory processes further guide the transformational changes, and if all three major functional elements align with the present live experiences then coachees are able to attain sustainable growth and development towards goal attainment.

It is expected that this new conceptual model will provide a strong supporting backbone for coaching psychology practice. This includes developmental measures both at the beginning and end of the coaching intervention for all elements described in this practitioner's model. Table 4.1 depicts the expected total functional changes from the application of the selective realism model.

Developmental issues and challenges

The inclusion of the neurological element in a single coaching intervention may pose a challenge, as it requires the sophisticated tools to identify and measure the specific regions of the brain activated and changed during coaching sessions. Coaching psychology is still not widely recognized as a scientific discipline for collaboration and joint application to support an individual's overall development. This can be a barrier to taking the initiative to seek collaboration from neuropsychology to facilitate coaching psychology practice using the selective realism conceptual model. Coaching psychology education is not yet included in the institutionalized practice delivering education for practice, for instance, for medical practice, which is delivered through medical schools in educational institutions. Coaching psychology practice is mainly privatized, and delivered by a single practitioner or a group of practitioners. As such, the cost-effectiveness of coaching psychology practice as a business is given more importance than the educational value inherent in coaching psychology. The presence of three functional elements in the conceptual model involves a costly intervention for which an institutionally driven practice is required. Furthermore, interdisciplinary collaboration and formally supported multi-agency delivery can enhance and strengthen an inclusive coaching psychology practice.

The proposed model provides the platform for this collaboration, which will be valuable to advance human science from the perspective of a coaching psychology scientific discipline.

Human behaviour is volatile and must be synthesized to manage and function effectively. The process involves all areas of human development to support the development of a fully functional individual. This is not an easy task. It requires teamwork and professional initiatives. The selective realism conceptual model in practice is one such initiative, and can provide a strong supportive foundation to enhance good practice in coaching psychology. It has been developed on the principles of realism and holism, and the active agency of an individual in their present environment. An individual's behavioural response occurs in relation to a stimulus or a collection of stimuli in the immediate environment, and the response is the result of interacting neurological and cognitive functioning processors and influenced by the immediate environment. The equation is BR = N + C x E (BR = behavioural response, N = neurological functions, C = cognitive functions and E = environment). The mathematical interpretation is if N = 5, C = 6 and E = 3 then BR = 33. The behavioural response can be an indicator of change and sustained progress on a scale from 0 to 100, with 100 representing the maximum level of change and achievement.

Neurological changes can be measured using the change magnitude of the specific region of the brain, as represented by 0 to 100, with 100 as the highest level of neuronal functions. Similarly, cognitive changes can be obtained using an appropriate measure or test with a score from 0 to 100, with 100 as the highest level of cognitive change. The rationale of assessing three major functional elements is that complex biological, psychological and cognitive functional elements determine an individual's reaction to the coaching environment. The emergence of selective realism can only be assessed through these three major functional elements, and this is expected to provide the scientific validity of this proposed new concept.

The value of a theoretical model supporting practical application and practice can only be ascertained when it is verified by the outcome. I hope practitioners will consider applying the selective realism conceptual model to their own coaching practice. This will then provide evidence-based support for this new practitioner's model for further development and application.

Conclusion

There seems to be a developmental delay in providing a strong theoretical foundation underpinning coaching psychology practice (Grant 2016). One of the developmental delays is attributed to positive and humanistic psychology. This concern can be addressed if coaching psychologists work to develop solid theoretical groundwork to support coaching psychology practice, and a differentiated but aligned disciplinary approach to deliver coaching psychology practice, armed with psychological key principles and fundamental constructs of human behaviour.

In this chapter, I have proposed a new paradigm for developing coaching psychology as an integrated scientific and practice-based discipline using a selective realism conceptual model for practice. The model emphasizes the fully functional capabilities of individuals to achieve their maximum potential, which can be nurtured and developed, changed and advanced using selective realism during the coaching intervention. The apparent complexity in this model can be simplified and made easier for administration if this is put into practice. The model is designed specifically for practitioners, and hence it has both theoretical and practical values.

Coaching psychology practice will soon be able to establish itself as an accredited professional practice, and will have a 'boost' or 'bumper' effect when it is supported by a distinctive theoretical arch and a practical model of practice. The selective realism coaching practitioner's model offers a practical model for practitioners to apply to their practice. This model is expected to advance knowledge about coaching psychology practice using a distinctive holistic approach and realism. It is hoped it will serve as a key guide and a companion reference point to maintain and improve professional coaching practice.

References

Boyatzis, R.E. (2006) An overview of intentional change from a complexity perspective, *Journal of Management Development*, 25(7): 607–23.

Boyatzis, R.E. and Akrivou, K. (2006) The ideal self as the driver of intentional change, *Journal of Management Development*, 25(7): 624–42.

Campion, J. (2011) Embracing neuroscience will keep us credible, *Coaching at Work*, 6(5): 11.

Cassidy, T. (2010) Holism in sports coaching: Beyond humanistic psychology, *International Journal of Sports Science & Coaching*, 5(4): 439–43.

Grant, A.M. (2015) Response to Dias et al.: Coaching the brain: Neuro-science or neuro-nonsense?, *The Coaching Psychologist*, 11(1): 21–7.

Grant, A.M. (2016) What can Sydney tell us about coaching? Research with implications for practice from down under, *Consulting Psychology Journal: Practice and Research*, 68(2): 105–17.

Grant, A.M., Curtayne, L. and Burton, G. (2009) Executive coaching enhances goal attainment, resilience, and workplace well-being: A randomised controlled study, *The Journal of Positive Psychology*, 4(5): 396–407.

Green, L.S., Oades, L.G. and Grant, A.M. (2006) Cognitive-behavioural, solution-focused life-coaching: Enhancing goal striving, well-being and hope, *Journal of Positive Psychology*, 1(3): 142–9.

Green, S., Grant, A.M. and Rynsaardt, J. (2007) Evidence-based life coaching for senior high school students: Building hardiness and hope, *International Coaching Psychology Review*, 2(1): 24–32.

Gregory, B.J. and Levy, E.P. (2012) Humanistic/person-centered approaches, in D.B. Peterson and T. Freire (eds) *The Wiley-Blackwell Handbook of the Psychology of Coaching and Mentoring*. Oxford: Wiley-Blackwell, pp. 283–97.

Greif, S. and Benning-Rohnke, E. (2015) Consistent implementation of goals through coaching, *Coaching Theory and Practice*, 1(1): 25–35.

Gyllensten, K., Palmer, S., Nilsson, E-K., Regnér, A.M. and Frodi, A. (2010) Experiences of cognitive coaching, *International Coaching Psychology Review*, 5(2): 98–108.
Hughes, J.L. (2002) Adjusting the mirror: Strategies for coaching executives with narcissistic personality features. Doctoral dissertation, Rutgers, the State University of New Jersey, Graduate School of Applied and Professional Psychology.
Mahoney, J.D. (2019) Self-awareness through the Johari window, *Training*, 56(5): 52.
Martin, L.S., Oades, L.G. and Caputi, P. (2012) What is personality change coaching and why is it important?, *International Coaching Psychology Review*, 7(2): 185–93.
Martin, L.S., Oades, L.G. and Caputi, P. (2014) Intentional personality change coaching: A randomised controlled trial of participant selected personality facet change using the Five-Factor Model of personality, *International Coaching Psychology Review*, 9(2): 182–95.
McCrae, R. and Costa, P.T. (2003) *Personality in Adulthood: A Five-Factor Theory Perspective*, 2nd edn. New York: Guilford Press.
Riddell, P. (2018) Coaching and neuroscience, in S. Palmer and A. Whybrow (eds) *Handbook of Coaching Psychology: A Guide for Practitioners*. New York: Routledge, pp. 14–24.
Rollnick, S., Mason, P. and Butler, C. (1999) *Health Behaviour Change: A Guide for Practitioners*. Edinburgh: Churchill Livingstone.
Schwartz, H.B., McFeeley B.M., Krivanek, T.J., Daffner, K.R. and Gale, S.A. (2019) The brain health champion study: Health coaching changes behaviours in patients with cognitive impairment, *Alzheimer's & Dementia*, 12(5): 771–9.
Shams, M. (2011) Conclusions and future directions, in M. Shams and D.A. Lane (eds) *Coaching in the Family Owned Business: A Path to Growth*. New York: Routledge, pp. 125–33.
Shams, M. (2015) Why is it important to understand the neurological basis of coaching intervention?, *The Coaching Psychologist*, 11(1): 28–9.
Shams, M. (2022) *Supporting the Family Business: A Coaching Practitioner's Handbook*, 2nd edn. New York: Routledge.

Part II

Application

Introduction

Part II aims to provide the platform to present appropriate knowledge of, and experiences in coaching psychology practice to understand, evaluate and optimize performance. It is hoped it will provide a valuable and useful resource for practitioners, academics, researchers, businesses, organizations, and all who are interested in applying coaching psychology to their respective areas.

In Part I, the context of practice, ethics in coaching psychology practice, and the theoretical basis of coaching psychology are presented, along with a new theoretical selective realism coaching psychology practice model. The chapters in Part II present evidence and practice-based discussions on the application of theories to effective coaching practice.

Part II will serve as a professional guide to support individuals to achieve optimum functioning and to increase their developmental lifeline. Each chapter in this part is written by expert coaching practitioners/coaching psychologists with the aim of providing learning impetus and a shared knowledge base to promote the application of coaching psychology. The distinctive feature of this part is the practical application of knowledge in relation to coaching psychology, and practice-related, evidence-based critical reflective discussions.

This part consists of six chapters. The discussion on the theoretical underpinning of coaching psychology practice is presented in Chapter 5, with examples from two different schools of thought – existential and gestalt influence on coaching practice. The discussion in this chapter provides further direction for the development of coaching psychology practice, which needs to be developed using relevant theoretical constructs and models. Chapter 6 takes an eclectic approach to offer a pluralistic model of coaching to acknowledge diversity and differences in individuals' functioning systems, and argues that individual differences should be reflected in coaching practice. One of the distinctive features of coaching psychology is that it addresses the coaching needs of specialists in different disciplines and other areas of psychology. Chapter 7 presents selected examples of psychology specialist subject areas to highlight the influence of coaching psychology practice on these areas. Using a coachee perspective to understand the effectiveness of coaching psychology practice, Chapter 8 provides an interesting discussion on coachee characteristics influencing the effectiveness of coaching outcomes.

Coaching psychology practice is evolving at an unpredictable period, subjected to continuous environmental changes and technological advances, so it is essential to have an update of its developmental progress in the light of these changes. An evaluative and persuasive discussion about practising coaching psychology in a changing society is presented in Chapter 9. Chapter 10 draws together the conclusions, using the key issues from each chapter, and presents emerging critical issues for further research and practice.

An existential and gestalt approach to group coaching

Tony Fusco and Toni Clarkson

Summary

This chapter explores the existential and gestalt approaches to coaching by looking at their application to group coaching leadership development. It examines both coaching approaches, as experienced by two coaches working with the same group, and considers what each approach achieves, why and how. It will look at the underlying theory of each approach and examine how existential and gestalt coaching, while both complementary in many ways, illuminate contrasting aspects of a group coaching process and the different individuals' experiences within the group.

Keywords: existential, gestalt, group coaching, leadership coaching, coaching psychology.

Introduction

Existential and gestalt coaching are both humanistic and non-directive approaches to coaching. Existential coaching is probably the most philosophical of approaches and engages coach and client in philosophical dialogue. By contrast, gestalt coaching is possibly the most egalitarian of approaches and has the equality of the coach and client relationship at its core. Neither existential nor gestalt coaching focuses too much on goal setting, action planning or performance improvement per se. Both are more concerned with a client's awareness and attitude towards life and their way-of-being.

Existential coaching focuses on the client's personal worldview, born from a culmination of their values and beliefs, and assumptions they have developed about the world and their place within it. Focusing on issues such as meaning, purpose and authenticity, existential coaching often leads to significant and profound changes within a person, but this comes as the result of a natural shift in their personal perspective and not because of directly targeted change. As we will see below, this indirect approach to change is known in gestalt psychology as 'paradoxical change'.

Of all coaching modalities, gestalt is probably the most non-directive and co-created. It holds at its core a coaching relationship that is built on the genuinely equal working alliance between coach and client. Described as 'an applied phenomenology' (Chidiac and Denham-Vaughan 2007), the ability of practitioners lies not in their mastery of tools and techniques to use with clients, but in their way of being with those clients. The use of awareness of self and other lies at the heart of gestalt coaching, and tools and techniques can interfere with the coach's ability to be with their client.

Both existential and gestalt coaching are interrelated and highly complementary, yet retain their own distinct styles and approaches which will become apparent throughout this chapter. By comparing two different forms of coaching, we hope the reader will get an appreciation for how both the coach's and coachee's experience of the same observed phenomena can be viewed and experienced in (at least) two different ways.

Aims

In this shared chapter one coach (Tony Fusco) takes an existentialist lens and the other (Toni Clarkson) takes a gestalt lens on the same shared experience of group coaching. We will outline the key tenets of both gestalt and existential coaching and then go on to give some examples from a shared group coaching case study we both facilitated. As coaches from differing disciplines, naturally we notice different things in the process. There is not the space in this chapter to discuss all aspects of each coaching approach, so this serves just as an introduction for those interested in the existential and gestalt coaching modalities.

Existential coaching

The existential coaching approach concerns itself with what it means to be human. It considers what human existence means in terms of our personal values, beliefs, attitudes, aspirations and identities – in sum, our way of being (Spinelli 2014). Its primary objective is to illuminate the client's fundamental worldview and orientation to the world regardless of the implicit or explicit coaching approach that is used to achieve that. Therefore, it is more attuned to how the client is being in their world rather than what they are doing or how they are performing (Spinelli and Horner 2008). The existentialist Emmy van Deurzen (2009) describes the existential project as more ontological than psychological in nature and says its purpose is to:

> help people to uncover the everyday mysteries in which they are enfolded and in which they may have become entangled. The process ... is intended to lead

> clients to greater awareness of where they find themselves in their lives, how they got there and where they want to go next. (van Deurzen 2009: 177)

Peltier (2011) makes the point that a key task of the existential coach is to help their client notice and reflect on both the choices they make and their pattern of choice-making – the aim being to help clients become more conscious and deliberate in their choice-making. To the coaching practitioner, particularly those new to the field, this may seem like a rather daunting blank page to work with, especially with no specific coaching framework or technique to use as a guide. There are, however, key reoccurring themes in existential philosophy and psychotherapy that can illuminate the path of existential coaching. These main concerns can vary slightly by name, but are often variations on the core existential themes summarized in Table 5.1.

Time – temporality/finitude/mortality

We are all beings that evolve through time. We all have a past, present and future that continue to influence and shape who we are. It is suggested we are never finished as beings but rather are always in the process of becoming-in-time (Heidegger 1962). However, awareness of this temporality can be problematic. As self-aware humans we can contemplate this passage of time and must grapple with the knowledge that it will end for us at some point. This insight leads inexorably to some of the other major concerns listed below. The main point from an existential perspective is that this inevitability should not prevent us from engaging meaningfully and purposefully with our lives. Indeed, it should encourage us. To paraphrase the existential psychotherapist Irvin Yalom (1980), though our physical death ends our life, the idea of death saves us. Somewhat paradoxically, the awareness of death can be what makes life worth living and can throw us fully into life.

Paradox – uncertainty/anxiety/absurdity

Although awareness of our finitude can give us an appetite for life, it can obviously create some tension also. If it is all temporary, we cannot help but wonder about the point of it all. This existential paradox can create a chasm of angst and a brooding sense of absurdity. How are we to live with the burden of such knowledge and live meaningful lives? The answer to this, from an existential

Table 5.1 Key existential concerns

Time	Temporality, finitude, mortality
Paradox	Uncertainty, anxiety, absurdity
Choice	Freedom, responsibility, passion
Meaning	Values, purpose, authenticity

perspective, is to accept life's paradox, angst and uncertainty and embrace the ontological project of your life. Assume full responsibility for it, make commitments and take actions. Simply put, decide upon and engage in choices because, from an existential perspective, your choices are who you are (Cox 2020). But accepting all of this, I am still left with the dilemma – what should I choose?

Choice – freedom/responsibility/passion

The responsibility of this freedom to make our own choices can itself be a huge existential burden and challenge. If I can really be the author of my own life, what should I do with it? If all eventually comes to nought, what should I choose, how should I choose? Many people inoculate themselves from the anxiety and angst of this burden by lapsing into a life of bad faith (Sartre 2001). That is, they ease this burden of responsibility and freedom of choice by following any number of predetermined life paths automatically laid out for them by the preordained authorities of culture, class, faith, family, tradition etc. A genuinely self-authored ontological project can be the most difficult of all projects, leading Jean-Paul Sartre (2001) to observe that we are 'condemned to freedom'.

Meaning – values/purpose/authenticity

This final category helps bring our existential project to life. It guides us towards what we fundamentally care about and what it is that we should be spending our finite time on earth doing. If I am able to accept the non-negotiable paradoxes and absurdities that come with being human, I am able to embrace my freedom of choice and take responsibility for deciding what will give my life meaningful form. What do I wholeheartedly want to commit my time and energies to? If I'm only here for a limited amount of time, and just the once (which most, though interestingly not all, existentialists believe), then I should make it count. So, my existential onto-dynamic project requires me to ask and answer that question, both of my life and to my life (Frankl 1985). And this I do by the committed application of my self-determined values to personally significant and meaningful life goals.

Existential tools and techniques

A useful coaching framework is to view the opportunities and predicaments of a coachee through the four dimensions of existence model (van Deurzen 2012). This is presented in Table 5.2.

The four existential domains focus on different aspects of existence as follows:

The physical dimension: This is the domain of the earth and nature. It includes our bodies, health and physical presence in the world. It also includes the sense we make of the interconnectedness of the world and the nature of both life and death.

Table 5.2 Four existential dimensions

Physical Life/death/environment/body/health	**Social** Relationships/belonging/communication
Psychological Thoughts/memories/identity/ freedom/self	**Spiritual** Intuition/values/ideas/meaning/purpose

The psychological dimension: This is the inner realm of who we are and how we have come to be. How do our life narratives form us and shape our beliefs, assumptions, ideals, hopes, fears and aspirations? It is here we construct our inner sense of individuality and selfhood.

The social dimension: Here exists our web of interconnections and relationships. It includes the time and place of our existence and all the interwoven demands, challenges and opportunities that it presents. Embedded amongst all of this is where we gain a sense of belonging and develop the relational and social aspect of our identity.

The spiritual dimension: This is the realm of our abstract life and where we establish our principles, ideologies, values and intuition. It is here that we construct the meaning of our lives and their every purpose. This is also where we try and make sense of the abstract realm of life that includes such concepts as truth, meaning, belonging or faith.

Each of these levels can connect and combine, as well as share tensions and paradoxes. It is the aim of the existential coach to examine each of these dimensions, exploring their overlaps and contradictions, and to bring each domain of the coachee's personal experience into greater focus (van Deurzen 2012). This is achieved with the use of observation and description, to draw attention to patterns and paradoxes, contrasts and contradictions. This also highlights blind spots, illusions or other distortions of reality that a coaching client may be living with. Clients are helped to explore the personal narrative they have built around their life, and to discover where this may no longer be a helpful interpretation and where and how it might need to be revisited, revised or even rewritten.

The ultimate goal of existential coaching is to help individuals to become more of who they naturally are (and can be). As such, it addresses one of the main themes in existential thought, that of personal authenticity (Mandic 2012). Existential authenticity asks a person to confront the reality of their life and such fundamental questions as 'have I taken full responsibility for my life and its choices?' and 'am I living a personally significant and meaningful life?' In leadership coaching, too, these fundamental questions emerge as central: 'have I taken full responsibility for my leadership and its choices?' and 'am I leading in a professionally (and personally) significant and meaningful way?' The four existential dimensions described above can also be used to frame authentic leadership development (Fusco et al. 2015), which serves as our group coaching case study below.

Gestalt coaching

As a practitioner rather than an academic, I (Toni Clarkson) focus on the relational aspect of gestalt. The responsibility we have as coaches is to hold the relationship in balance with the truthfulness of our immediate experience. I am minded that writing about gestalt is similar to trying to describe a scent to someone who has not experienced it before. Put simply, you have to experience it. While the theory can help us build a framework for our practice, 'Praxis is the process by which theory becomes animated in the actions of its adherents' (Brownell 2010: 6).

Like existentialism, gestalt does not focus on the creation of goals, but enables the client to become more sharply aware of what is. This leans into Beisser's (1970) theory of 'paradoxical change' where he posits that change only occurs when we have a grasp and acceptance of what really is – awareness being the goal as opposed to actions and plans. Gestalt coaches are awareness agents and not change agents. We do not interpret, diagnose or lead – we co-inquire. This focus on mutual exploration of the here and now in creating awareness makes gestalt one of the liveliest and most dynamic of all the coaching modalities. It lives and moves.

In addition to the importance of the relationship and the humanistic beliefs that underpin most coaching and therapy, additional key constructs for the gestalt coach include the following.

Dialogue

Originally introduced by Martin Buber (1965), dialogue, rather than discussion, is central to the effectiveness of the gestalt coaching dyad. According to Buber, dialogue occurs 'neither in one of the two partners, nor in both together, but only in their dialogue itself, in the "between" in which they live together' (Buber 1965: 75). In such dialogue the coach holds back on their theories, directiveness, hypotheses and expertise, and instead engages with their client as an equal. The coach is open to and interested in the client's experience but does not guide it.

Hycner and Jacobs (1995: xi) describe dialogue as 'an attitude and awareness and openness about caring about the unique other person and our interhuman connectedness with that person … an attitude of genuinely feeling/sensing/experiencing the other persons as a person (not an object or a part-object), and a willingness to "hear" the other person's experience without pre-judgment'.

Holism

Gestalt coaching rejects the Cartesian split of mind and body. It believes maintaining the link between mind and body gives access to important information and awareness. Gestalt coaching asks both coach and client to access information from both of these sources in order to reach more deep, meaningful and vivid experience in the moment.

Here and now

Gestalt coaching places particular emphasis on exploring the 'here and now'. Coaches often find that clients can tend to be elsewhere – creating stories and imaginings of the past and future without a clear grasp on the coordinates of the present. When this happens, it is almost impossible to work out a map for the journey ahead. Sensate and cognitive information can be most keenly experienced now. Reactions to thoughts and feelings about our past or future experience occur in the here and now. While past patterns and future intentions clearly matter, gestalt coaching focuses on what is being experienced by both coach and client in the moment.

Experimentation

Many coaching modalities involve 'experimentation' in some form, for example, constellation work, metaphors, artefacts, art or movement. But what distinguishes gestalt experimentation is the originality and emergence of the experiment. The purpose of the experiment is to enable the client to experience a more somatic and deeper perspective of their current situation, to mine more data by moving away from the tangle of pure cognitive experience. Thus, an experiment – which the client is always invited and not requested to participate in – is one that is created in the moment. It is not prepared in advance or pulled out of the metaphorical toolbox. Coaches share the experiment with the client, and enquire as to their experience of it, their insights and reactions.

Phenomenology

Originated by Edmund Husserl (1931), phenomenology is the study of how we perceive the phenomena we are conscious of. For example, as a coach I may notice that I feel confused when my client describes a situation they are facing; I may notice a tightness in my throat when they speak about something important to them. Husserl put forward three main skills to use in the observation of phenomena:

- Horizontalism: where we do not ascribe any hierarchy of importance to what we notice.
- Bracketing: putting aside our hypotheses about the situation, our own prior experience and preconceptions.
- Description: describing what we are noticing without interpretation.

Sharing our own phenomenology and inquiring into the client's allows a more vivid and in-depth exploration and investigation into the here and now.

Gestalt tools and techniques

As noted above, gestalt coaching is more about presence, awareness and dialogue than it is about tools. However, there are some background frameworks

Figure 5.1 The gestalt Cycle of Experience

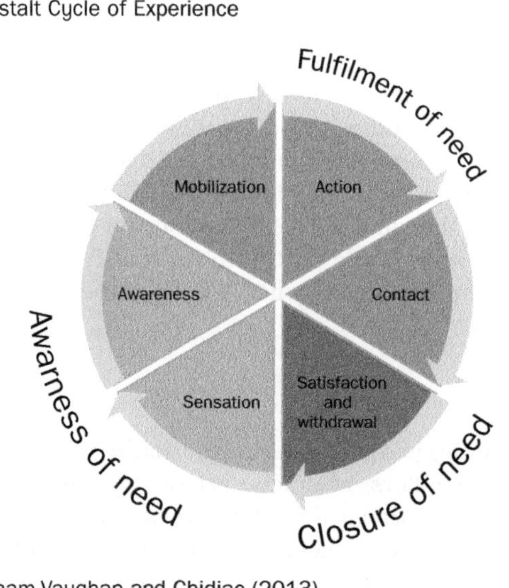

Adapted from Denham-Vaughan and Chidiac (2013).

that can help us work with our clients, for example, the Cycle of Experience (Figure 5.1) and the SOS model (Figure 5.2) on p. 68.

The Cycle of Experience

Central to gestalt coaching is the Cycle of Experience (Zinker 1977). The stages of the cycle represent the flow of our process in satisfying our needs; in many situations we are in contact or 'flow', and the cycle naturally completes itself. However, in coaching situations we are often working with interruptions to this flow that our client is experiencing.

- Sensation: For example, I notice that my mouth is dry, and my throat feels tight.
- Awareness: If I stay with this sensation long enough, I may recognize that I am thirsty.
- Mobilization: I gather my energy and focus to satisfy this need by choosing a drink.
- Action: I act on my need and get the drink.
- Contact: I drink it.
- Satisfaction and withdrawal: I spend enough time to recognize that the drink has allayed my thirst and that I don't need to drink any more. I can move on to the next thing.

Looking at the example above, what if I did not take enough notice of my initial sensation? What if I mistook my thirst for a sore throat, or ignored the sensation entirely? The 'need' would not go away but my actions – and indeed plans or goals – would be misdirected.

At any point on the cycle, we have the potential for interruptions to flow, sometimes from familiar patterns of response, from 'unfinished business' from the past, or the context of our current situation. I might, for instance, decide that the needs or perceived expectations of others are more important and pressing than my own, and delay or stop my own contact. My need doesn't go away, but it is subsumed in other action and contact. It should be noted here that the interested reader may wish to inquire further into the 'moderations of contact' that accompany the different stages on the Cycle of Experience, as there is not the space in this chapter to introduce each of them.

While the simple example of thirst and a drink serves to illustrate the cycle, our work as coaches involves more complex situations to which this cycle is applied. This is demonstrated by an illustrative example with a recent client.

An example

A female director in a City law firm wanted to work on her 'presentation style and content' to the Partners in the monthly meeting. She was firm that the Partners were disinterested in what she presented and so she hated the sessions. She wanted to make her content more interesting or find a way to feel less intimidated. Based on this perspective or 'Awareness', her Cycle of Experience followed an interrupted, uncomfortable pattern which was actually out of her Awareness. Some co-inquiry revealed that she is confident, able and comfortable when presenting to her international team or her peers. Rather than take this 'awareness' as being the full picture, an experiment presented itself for us to try. I invited her to stand outside the room where the Partners' meetings take place, laptop under arm, ready for the monthly meeting, and to take time to notice what she became aware of, and then to walk in, sit and present as she would usually do. I remained inside. I shared my phenomenology of her walk in (I felt ignored, I didn't notice her after she sat down and felt my interest drift). I shared my phenomenology of her presentation (I felt excluded, low energy and couldn't remember what she said, and quickly wanted to engage with my own computer). She started laughing. She said almost instantly outside the door she realized what was happening, and she described what I have translated to the cycle below. It is briefly like this:

- Sensation: Aware only of feeling foolish and boring in the meetings. Tries to ignore the internal sensation of dread in her stomach which stresses her, but it builds up inside.
- Awareness: 'They are not interested in my function and our activities.'
- Mobilization: Anticipation for meeting filled with anxiety and ignores that the meeting is happening. Lots of procrastination.
- Action: Minimal preparation of facts with accompanied thoughts of 'it will be awful'.
- Contact: Walking in as close to start as possible; hunched over and without making eye contact, sitting in least observable place; monotone voice,

screen staring. Not fully 'present' in the meeting, just going through what is necessary and trying to get it over with.
- Satisfaction and withdrawal: Rushing to the next task with only relief that this is over for a month.

Her deepened and changed experience and connection with the embodied experience led to a new awareness which flowed without any coaching on action plans, activities, goals or timescales. In fact, the whole experiment to changed awareness took 15 minutes:

- Sensation: Internal energy, positivity and agency. Feeling of standing straight and looking forward.
- New awareness: How she currently walks in, sits and presents makes it boring and disconnecting for the partners. She wants them to be interested.
- Mobilization: Anticipation for meeting filled with energy and excitement.
- Action: Greater preparation of material and looking forward to sharing with all.
- Contact: Walking in upright, making eye contact, smiling and speaking; sitting prominently; looking at people directly when presenting and using names/ functions. Present, alive and focused.
- Satisfaction and withdrawal: Staying with the satisfaction of a good meeting, feeling appreciated and respected and taking credit.

Self-other-situation (SOS)

The concept of holism in gestalt is based on the idea that our behaviour and experience are affected by and connected to the context we operate in. I am always me, but a different me in differing situations, some of which may be in conflict with my needs. Fritz Perls (1973: 16) describes this as 'the individual can exist only in an environmental field. The individual is inevitably, at every

Figure 5.2 The SOS model

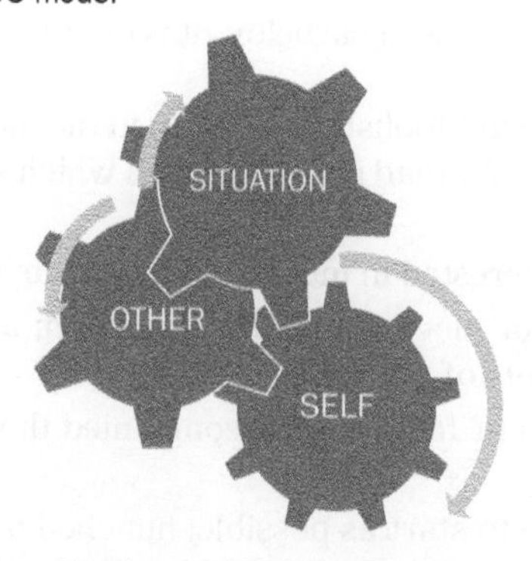

Adapted from Denham-Vaughan and Chidiac (2013).

moment, a part of some field, which includes both him and his environment. The nature of the relationship between him and his environment determines the human being's behaviour.'

Denham-Vaughan and Chidiac (2013) created the SOS model (Self, Other and Situation) which encourages the coach to explore and hold three areas when working with the client (Figure 5.2). As practitioners, we explore with our clients what we are conscious of in all three areas in their here and now. Denham-Vaughan and Chidiac suggest that our ethical presence as a practitioner lies in the intersection of all three areas when working with a client.

Leadership group coaching case study

The case study we have chosen is a group coaching approach to authentic leadership development (ALD), as authenticity is a key concern of both existential and gestalt coaching as well as desirable in leadership. Two particular features make this group-format ALD approach existential in nature. The first is the inclusion of the four world dimensions described above: the physical, social, psychological and spiritual dimensions. Second, is the temporal coaching structure that is orientated along a past/present/future perspective. This is based on the insight that humans are fundamentally temporal beings who exist first and foremost in time, constantly forming and influenced by their future as well as their past.

Group coaching is also a rich gestalt environment. The role of gestalt coaching is to create the space for people to become more aware of who they are, both as a leader and an individual. It focuses on them as themselves, rather than who or what they believe they are expected to become. As leadership is a fundamentally social enterprise it makes the group coaching environment particularly powerful from a gestalt perspective.

Day 1: the past and life narratives

Each of the four existential domains and the perspectives of past/present/future of course all overlap and inform each other, meaning the temporal issues of time and finitude are ever-present. Although gestalt's focus on the here and now might imply a disinterest in the past or future perspective of this format, its approach enables self-inquiry in the moment to the experience participants have when looking both backwards and forwards. The past is focused on memories and the future on imaginings, whereas the present is focused on genuine reactions and real experience. We can only be 'aware' in the now. Thus, gestalt brings the 'there-and-then' into the 'here and now'.

On Day 1, participants are asked to present their life narrative to the coaching group. In doing so they address the first half of van Deurzen's ontologically informed existential project that is intended to 'lead clients to greater awareness of where they find themselves in their lives and how they got there'. Asking individuals to look at their past, their present and then their future helps them view their life in the round and begin the second part of the existential project which, after looking at how they got where they are, is to consider 'where they might want to go next'.

Constructing and presenting their life stories force individuals to assess and plot their being-in-time and an estimation of progress along their life trajectory. This is very much situated within their physical existential dimension, but also leads them to reflect on the spiritual dimension – their overall sense of meaning in their lives and their leadership careers. One senior manager from a 2021 group made the following self-observation:

> *I very rarely take the time to pause, take stock and think deeply about anything. I don't spend enough time being truly present with myself and my thoughts. I have lots of questions that remain unanswered because I supress them or don't take the time to really understand them.*

Phenomenology: From a gestalt perspective my focus was not so much on this person's past but on my own phenomenology in the here and now as they talked through their lifeline. I noticed that something shifted in the field at a particular point when they were sharing how they had moved about, and their family had changed. Their voice became quieter and more hesitant, their eye contact dropped, and they caught their breath. I started to feel a little lost and sad at this point, and said so. They replied that this was the time in their life when they started to feel dislocated and isolated. I asked what they were aware of right now, to which they replied that they were aware of not belonging, and of needing to. It felt like an important moment. It created some space for awareness.

Now consider the following passage from the same individual after presenting their life narrative to the group:

> *There was something quite confronting about talking about my life's highs and lows out loud which left me with a bit of a vulnerability hangover! The exercise, combined with the observations and questions from the group, threw up some big questions for me around the meaning of belonging, why it is so important to me, and who I am when I belong versus who I am otherwise and which of those versions is authentically me. I have come to realize that when I belong, I am authentically me. There's a level of security and acceptance that comes as part of feeling that I truly belong that allows me to treat my own needs with equal importance. It has also provoked some thought about my boundaries and how I position myself and has also driven a greater need to truly understand my purpose. I have come to realize that my purpose as a leader is to ensure people have what they need to thrive. This is me at my best and when I think about what the future holds for me career-wise, I realize that I need to find a path that aligns with that because that's what will truly fulfil me.*

This exercise sews a thread through a person's entire past/present/future. The existential spiritual domain identifies the person's purpose, in life and leadership, and clarifies the key values that guide that purpose.

Day 2: the present and leadership temperament

Day 2 moves the coaching group participants along their timeline into the present and situates them in the psychological existential dimension. They explore the impact of their assessed leadership temperaments, how these serve them well and where this challenges them. Unlike more superficial leadership personality assessments, such 'onto-dynamic reflection' is not always easy or straightforward, as one participant stated:

> *I think I am a traditional leader focused very much on the here and now, which means strategy, change and innovation aren't really strength areas for me. So, I have to wonder if I can be the leader I authentically am, in a world that demands change, strategic thinking and innovation?*

This work in the psychological dimension also influences the social domain, as people working with these leaders eventually experience and benefit from the leader's behaviour change – change that comes about because of their internal shifts in beliefs and assumptions about their own way-of-being. This multi-domain, broad time perspective coaching approach can bring startling clarity to individuals. As one leader succinctly summarized:

> *The whole process has helped build my awareness of my skills and competencies. But most importantly it has also helped me understand what I care most about. It has shone light into new areas and has pushed me to understand truths that were hidden in plain sight!*

The inclusion of a psychometric assessment on Day 2 creates some interesting tension with gestalt practice. Given the level of focus and meaning that gestalt places on the subjective awareness of self – both cognitive and somatic – the introduction of an external psychometric 'objectivity', that 'tells you what you are like', has the potential for interference into the client's awareness in terms of both holism and context. In over 20 years of practice each, we have noticed a polarization in people's response to psychometrics – either a wholesale rejection or, more frequently, a wholesale acceptance of everything in their report. This willingness to either 'spit' or 'swallow' without 'chewing' can potentially interfere with the genuine examination of the lived experience of the client.

To create space for some mitigation against this somewhat binary response, we introduce the psychometric as part of the participant's 'Context' ('Situation' in the SOS model) rather than the 'Self' lens. By metaphorically separating it in this way, we place temperament as part of the participant's field, something that can influence how we behave along with other events, but something we have choice over once we are aware – we do not place it as the definition of who they are. We encourage each participant to notice how they respond to key aspects of their reported leadership temperament; to notice their embodied reaction and to see what lands and stays with them and what they reject. This can lead to some interesting awareness, for example:

> *It became clear why I struggled with certain parts of my job, and absolutely loved other areas. This has directly led me to increase my delegation at work as I pass on tasks much better suited to other temperament types, which allows me to focus on what I'm best at. This approach of sharing has improved efficiency, teamwork and morale significantly.*

Also,

> *It has profoundly changed my views on my own capabilities and potential. I have more confidence in my views now I have re-examined them so thoroughly. The output has really challenged the path my career has taken to date, but I'm using the insight to help me understand how I change things going forward.*

Day 3: the future and SOS

Day 3 of the coaching situates the group very much in their future and social domains. The participants' learning takes place through the gestalt group coaching SOS exercise described above. Group members bring in a leadership issue of concern, usually involving some element of uncertainty and ambiguity. They are asked to consider their challenge from the three distinct Self-Other-Situation perspectives and are once again coached by the group. This never fails to broaden their perspective of the challenge, increasing their insight, understanding and awareness. From this, ideas for the way forward always naturally emerge.

Gestalt experimentation

In one session, a participant was talking about a new organization and role they were moving to, and while on 'Situation' they started to speak about how their 'gremlin' heightened their anxiety about the new role. I noticed they looked to and put their hand on their right shoulder and made a pained expression when speaking about this gremlin. I reflected this back to them, and they said that this gremlin had been present their whole life. We spent some time exploring why the gremlin was located on their right shoulder (to whisper continually in their ear), and how it felt (heavy). As they were about to move to the 'Other' chair, I invited them to try an experiment: to place the gremlin in the 'Other' chair and have a conversation with it, exploring the needs and perspectives of the gremlin along with their own. This is how this individual summed up their experience:

> *The challenge from the group about evicting my 'gremlin' was an enormously helpful challenge because the process of stepping into 'Other' (in this instance the gremlin) totally shifted how I felt about it. For so long it has felt like a heavy weight on my back that at times has led me to feel quite claustrophobic, but I physically felt a movement in response to my gratitude and compassion for this thing that has served and protected me so well for so long. I felt its sadness at not*

feeling needed in the same way and was quite overwhelmed by an urge to comfort it and reassure it that it still has a role to play but an evolved one. I have spent so many years doubting myself and comparing myself to others in a professional capacity that the work we have done to understand ourselves as authentic leaders has provided me with a newfound confidence in who I am, what I bring to the table and how I can have an impact. I want to go into my new role aligned to my values so that the leader my colleagues experience is authentically me.

An experiment which involves the somatic, the cognitive and the here and now can create a deeper and richer perspective on 'what is' for the client and, having fully explored the Sensations and the flow to Awareness through the Cycle of Experience can bring transformational clarity. However, we need to temper our own desire as coaches to 'move the client' along and ensure we stay with their experience in the moment. Carlson and Kolodny (2009) refer to such presence with clients as 'meeting them where they are rather than aiming them towards where we think they should be'. They furthermore discuss that as practitioners we often believe we are being helpful and skilful by sharing our insights and hypotheses with our client, but this is significantly less useful and powerful than when we stay where the client is and share with them our own phenomenological experience.

Conclusion

As Spinelli and Horner (2008) comment, the existential approach to coaching is reflective, exploratory and deeply challenging. It is best suited to clients who want to explore and understand the complexities of their lives. Paradox, conflict, uncertainty and ambiguity are all facts of life that can benefit from existential exploration. Such areas might include the search for meaning in a coaching client's life/career or trying to determine and understand their personal and professional values. Trying to understand your personal values and purpose, and what you want to achieve with your life requires a bold confrontation with your own personal existence. As such, the existential approach to coaching is particularly helpful for those facing significant change in their personal or professional life such as career change, role transition, promotion or retirement. It is perhaps less suitable for individuals who are looking for concrete outcomes, measurable performance increases or other such certainties. It encourages us to embrace the uncertainty of being human (and the anxiety that evokes) which in turn helps us to tolerate it and make sense of it. Change of a person's being-in-the-world inevitably follows, which in turn results in positive and demonstrable shifts in how they engage with themselves, others and their professional endeavours. But this change is paradoxical. It does not result from a behaviour-focused or goal-orientated coaching intervention but occurs naturally as a result of increased levels of awareness, insight and understanding.

From the gestalt perspective there are a myriad of choice points for the practitioner in every coaching conversation we have; the here and now with the client, our own epistemology, praxis and experience shape which of those choice points we attend to and how we choose to react in every instance. Thus, Husserl's bracketing remains more of an aim than a reality, and of course a point to debate; Both gestalt and existentialism share a philosophical lens that places the client at the centre of their own will, and trust that the client knows best and is in that sense self-righting. Existentialism focuses on individuals' important meta-questions that may have roots embedded in the individual's time domains of their past, present or future. Gestalt works with what is live and emergent for the client, focusing on the here and now, both somatic and cognitive.

If we were to summarize one all-encompassing outcome from both the existential and the gestalt approach, it would probably be that of personal authenticity: the acknowledgement and acceptance of the key concerns of choice, freedom and what is; to become fully aware of the facts of our life and to accept that we have ultimate control of these facts, or at least our perception and reaction to them. As summed up by one particular group member, 'I feel energized and more in control of my life now and the changes I want to make in it.' It is worth re-emphasizing one last time that such shifts in awareness and intent as noted above come not from action-orientated, goal-focused coaching, but from awareness-coaching and the paradoxical change inherent in both existential and gestalt coaching.

References

Beisser, A.R. (1970) The paradoxical theory of change, in J. Fagan and I.L. Shepherd (eds) *Gestalt Therapy Now*. New York: Harper & Row, pp. 77–80.

Brownell, P. (2010) *Gestalt Therapy: A Guide to Contemporary Practice*. New York: Springer

Buber, M. (1965) *The Knowledge of Man: A Philosophy of the Interhuman* (trans. M.S. Friedman and R.G. Smith). New York: Harper & Row.

Carlson, C. and Kolodny, R. (2009) Embodying field theory in how we work with groups and large systems, in D. Ullman and G. Wheeler (eds) *Co-Creating the Field: Intention and Practice in the Age of Complexity*. Santa Cruz, CA: Gestalt Press, p. 147.

Chidiac, M. and Denham-Vaughan, S. (2007) The process of presence: Energetic availability and fluid responsiveness, *British Gestalt Journal*, 16(1): 9–19.

Cox, G. (2020) *How to Be an Existentialist*. London: Bloomsbury Academic.

Denham-Vaughan, S. and Chidiac, M. (2013) SOS: A relational orientation towards social inclusion, *Mental Health and Social Inclusion*, 17(2): 100–7.

Frankl, V.E. (1985) *Man's Search for Meaning*. New York: Simon & Schuster.

Fusco, T., O'Riordan, S. and Palmer, S. (2015) An existential approach to authentic leadership development: A review of the existential coaching literature and its relationship to authentic leadership, *The Coaching Psychologist*, 11(2): 61–71.

Heidegger, M. (1962) *Being and Time* (trans. J. Macquarrie and E. Robinson). New York: Harper.

Husserl, E. (1931) *General Introduction to Pure Phenomenology* (trans. W.R. Boyce Gibson). London: George Allen and Unwin.

Hycner, H. and Jacobs, L. (1995) *The Healing Relationship in Gestalt Therapy*. New York: Gestalt Journal Press.

Mandic, M. (2012) Authenticity in existential coaching, in E. van Deurzen and M. Hanaway (eds) *Existential Perspectives on Coaching*. Basingstoke: Palgrave Macmillan, pp. 3–20.
Peltier, B. (2011) *The Psychology of Executive Coaching: Theory and Application*. New York: Taylor & Francis.
Perls, F. (1973) *The Gestalt Approach and the Eyewitness to Therapy*. Palo Alto, CA: Science and Behaviour Books.
Sartre, J.P. (2001) *Being and Nothingness: An Essay in Phenomenological Ontology*. New York: Citadel Press.
Spinelli, E. (2014) Existential coaching, in E. Cox, T. Bachkirova and D.A. Clutterbuck (eds) *The Complete Handbook of Coaching*, 2nd edn. London: Sage, pp. 91–103.
Spinelli, E. and Horner, C. (2008) An existential approach to coaching psychology, in S. Palmer and A. Whybrow (eds) *Handbook of Coaching Psychology: A Guide for Practitioners*. Abingdon: Routledge, pp. 118–32.
van Deurzen, E. (2009) *Everyday Mysteries: A Handbook of Existential Psychotherapy*. Abingdon: Routledge.
van Deurzen, E. (2012) The existential ideology and framework for coaching, in E. van Deurzen and M. Hanaway (eds) *Existential Perspectives on Coaching*. Basingstoke: Palgrave Macmillan, pp. 3–20.
Yalom, I. (1980) *Existential Psychotherapy*. New York: Basic Books.
Zinker, J. (1977) *Creative Process in Gestalt Therapy*. New York: Brunner/Mazel Publishers.

Pluralistic coaching: Building bespoke process

Bruce Grimley

Summary

This chapter looks at coaching psychology from a pluralist perspective. Pluralism has at its heart the belief that any significant question can be answered in a variety of legitimate ways (Rescher 1993). Practitioner coaches who adopt this modality have a preference for diversity over uniformity and multiplicity over unity (McLennan 1995) as well as pragmatism over idealism (James 1996). Pluralist thinking goes back to the pre-Socratic philosophers, who held that the basic elements of Earth, Air, Fire and Water together constituted the basis of scientific knowledge; this was contrasted with the monistic metaphysical view that in fact there was another singular explanation, beyond physics and these basic elements, which underpinned scientific endeavour. Similarly, pluralistic coaches believe that the diversity of human nature cannot be reduced to a single principle. As each person is different, clients should not be tied to a Procrustean bed, but rather the coach should be conversant with a number of theoretical approaches and the associated methods and techniques which flow from them, so as to meet the needs of each coachee. This chapter explores how a variety of psychological approaches can be woven together, as demonstrated by the author in his practice of 25 years, with reference to a case history and his own pluralist model.

Keywords: coaching practice, coaching psychology models, coaching practitioners, ego state, context, experiential, rapport, 7C's, structure, process, excellence.

Introduction

Pluralistic theory in practice believes that coaching is always co-coaching, and client–coach collaboration is a key dynamic, with an understanding that each new coachee is totally unique. The coachee indeed is the best person to provide the coach with the information they need to generate successful momentum and theoretical as well as practical orientation. Pluralism takes a postmodern perspective (McLennan 1995), and the research of Pendle (2015) suggests a number of benefits of a pluralist perspective specifically in coaching:

1 Structure
2 An enriched sense of professional identity
3 A renewed energy for professional development
4 The desirability of blending different approaches.

The structure for a pluralist approach is provided by Cooper and McLeod (2010), who insist that each intervention must be subsumed by goals, tasks and methods. Indeed, Grimley (2019) argues that any coaching intervention must have sound construct validity and demonstrate that this structure is related to meaningful coaching outcomes.

Aims

This chapter aims to present a pluralistic perspective towards coaching. In attempting to fill the void concerning theoretical orientation, it offers a narrative of the author's own 25 years of experience in coaching psychology. During this time he has built his own theory of coaching, drawing from the psychological literature, his own experience and feedback from clients, and publishing these ideas for consideration by others for further peer review (Grimley 2013, 2015, 2016, 2021a, 2021b).

Key questions

Where does pluralism come from and what is its basic premise?

In answering this question it is best to step back and understand why and how pluralism came into existence in modern practice, despite having been in existence since the pre-Socratic philosophers. Pluralism is effectively a reaction against 'schoolism' and the weakness of unitary models of theory and practice. In addressing this, Cooper and McLeod (2007) cite (Wampold 2001), who suggests that no single approach has a superior grasp of the truth.

Miller et al. (1997) attempted to find out which approach works best, and found there is an equivalence effect – the pervasive finding is that different models are equally and relatively ineffective, with the basic principles of rapport and client resourcefulness being the two independent variables that account for 70 per cent of outcome success. They found only 15 per cent of outcome success is attributed to psychological models.

In the modern research landscape, however, despite these well-known findings there is an equally pervasive tendency for outcome research to be dominated by an agenda to 'prove' the relative superiority of competing unitary models, which, in the minds of Cooper and McLeod (2007), is a futile endeavour.

What Cooper and McLeod (2011) do is provide both a philosophical foundation and a structural framework within which to organize interventions. Pendle (2015) points out this enables the practitioner to avoid both the rigidity of schoolism on the one hand, and 'wild eclecticism' on the other, which can be characterized as 'flying by the seat of your pants, grabbing wildly at whatever comes to hand' (Hollanders 2000: 38).

Which theories should I choose from when acting as a pluralist coach?

This is a very personal decision for the practising coach. However, in order to supplement the growing pluralist literature, it should sit within the framework provided by Cooper and McLeod (2011). This has at the top the interdependent variables of goals, tasks and methods. As can be seen by the multiplicity of keywords at the head of this chapter, because people are different, very often the pluralist coach needs a widely differentiated set of tools from a variety of theoretical perspectives to address this difference and the iconic question of Gordon Paul (1969: 44): 'What treatment, by whom, is most effective for this individual with that specific problem, and under which set of circumstances?' As would also be expected in a pluralist approach, to answer this question a variety of research methods are used without a hierarchy of evidence. Number-based methods (quantitative), word-based methods (qualitative), case studies, outcome studies, surveys and experimental designs all have something equally useful to contribute. What is also important to recognize in pluralist coaching is that as a coach develops their own pluralist approach, they should not begin to favour one theory over others in their work and unintentionally drift back into the unitary model mindset.

The integrative or eclectic approaches are increasingly becoming more popular, and some would say in the profession of psychotherapy this is now the most common theoretical orientation (Norcross 2005). However, Cooper and McLeod (2011) notice, as already mentioned, that despite deriving from a variety of theoretical and technical approaches, this popular approach ends up becoming very similar to unitary models. They give as examples cognitive analytical theory (Ryle 1990), the problem management approach (Egan 1994) and the multi-modal perspective (Lazarus 1981, 2005), which are all cited by Downing (2004). A pluralistic approach to coaching is an integrative approach which avoids the tendency to develop over time in such a way that what is integrated becomes a new unitary model, imposing upon the client a particular way of working that does an injustice to the client–coach collaboration. This is achieved through adopting the philosophical construct of pluralism, rather than a variety of psychological constructs. It also requires the coach to commit to a sustained engagement with the client's view of what will be helpful for them.

In the specific case of the author, a move towards the diversity of pluralism was instigated by the observation over ten years of coaching practice and reflection on case notes that clients behaved and presented in very different ways on different occasions. This presentation depended on the context they were in, and the work of Jung on unconscious complexes seemed to be a very useful explanatory framework for this observation (Grimley 2005: 2–4). Indeed Jung pointed out that complexes are splinter psyches, and they behave like independent beings (Samuels 1985: 49).

Formalizing the differences triggered in different contexts and the development of the 7C's model of coaching

Central to a pluralistic approach is the client–coach collaboration. While working as both a coach and therapist during 1995 to 2005 the author, in seeking to understand the goals of his clients and collaboratively generating appropriate tasks using basic cognitive behavioural coaching (CBC) methods, such as Socratic questioning, goal setting, reframing and tasking, discovered for himself a set of variables, all beginning with the letter C (Figure 6.1), which seemed to be central to the coaching endeavour (Grimley 2002).

However, he discovered as he continued in practice that very often a kind of resistance to satisfying some of the C's occurred. This was important, because in developing 7C's the author began to think every one of the variables beginning with C needed to be addressed. If only six were addressed and the client was released, then the lack of ecology, evidenced by the missing C, would mean the solution would not be sustainable in the long term, and a return to default functioning would eventually occur. For instance, in executive coaching

Figure 6.1 7C's coaching

Coaching

Process variables

- Clarity
- Confidence/Congruence
- Capability
- Creativity/Courage
- Commitment
- Climate
- Communication

Content variables

- Context of you and:
- People very close to you
- Work colleagues
- Interpersonal skills
- Career
- Money
- Health
- Relaxation

Sexy Variables. Rapport Journal. Summer 2002.

Sailing the 7 C's of Courage. *AC Bulletin* Summer 2005.

a client had tremendous difficulty in Committing to an agreed outcome with enthusiasm. They were very Clear, they could Communicate what they wished with Confidence, and they were incredibly Capable and Creative with the Climate being right. But despite this there was something missing which prevented total Commitment to the outcome. However, in talking with this very same client in coaching concerning their family – i.e. in a different context – they had no difficulty at all in addressing each of the 7C process variables. In the context of their career the client was literally a different person, who was missing the competency of being able to commit to a particular and necessary task, compared to who they were in the context of family where they were fulfilled, functioning and living in a flow-like state (Csikszentmihalyi 1990).

Development of 'Core Code'

This presentation of a 'different' person in a different context piqued the author's curiosity and he developed a questionnaire named 'Core Code' to provide a sense of the client's well-being along well-known components of stress. The definition of stress coined by Cooper and Palmer (2000) was extended for this purpose: 'Stress occurs when expectations exceed a person's perception of capability in an area of extreme importance' (Grimley 2005). Woven into the 26-item questionnaire, however, were eight particular contexts which the author had noticed as being significant and important when reflecting on case notes:

1 Relationship with the self
2 Career
3 Relationship with people very close (intimate others)
4 Relationship with people at work
5 Money
6 Health
7 Ability to relax and unwind
8 Interpersonal skills

The author conducted a principal components analysis (PCA) on two separate sets of data (N = 200) in both 2005 and 2017. The participants were self-selecting professionals with an interest in continuing professional development (CPD), and the 26-item questionnaire was completed online. What the author was curious to find out was whether any one of the eight context variables above was significantly related to the experience of stress. What he found in each of the analyses was a one-factor solution, and the only one of the eight context variables within this factor was the coachee's relationship with themselves. Each of the items in this one-factor solution also co-varied with the participant's experience of stress. In developing goals and setting tasks, then, various methods within coaching which support the coachee's fundamental relationship with

Table 6.1 One-factor solution (PCA) of 7C's model

1	I feel very good about myself every day of the week (0.72)
2	When I think of my future, I can see many exciting tasks to be accomplished (0.74)
3	I often take corrective action when my life does not go according to plan (0.71)
4	I am very sure of myself (0.71)
5	I am confident I have what it takes to achieve my goals in life (0.78)

Source: Grimley (2005)

Table 6.2 Replication of PCA of 7C's model (2017)

1	When I think of my future, I can see many exciting tasks to be accomplished (0.77)
2	I feel I control my destiny (0.75)
3	I often take corrective action when my life does not go according to plan (0.73)
4	I am very sure of myself (0.73)
5	I very rarely feel anxious (0.72)
6	I am confident I have what it takes to achieve my goals in life (0.78)

Source: Grimley (2020)

themselves were seen as pivotal to this developing model of pluralist coaching. The author had seen how in one context the coachee was fine, yet in another context they could not address the complete set of process 7C's. Coaching therefore needed to identify first of all the specific context in which the coachee wished to excel, and then target their fundamental relationship to themselves within that context. The results of the PCA with loadings into the one-factor solution in 2005 and 2017 can be seen above in Tables 6.1 and 6.2.

Digging deeper: the addition of further theoretical perspectives

As mentioned above, what piqued the author's interest was how clients could present in one context as being in a flow type of state and then as soon as the coaching conversation turned to the area of concern, transform in front of him to somebody who lacked belief and capability. For some reason they had become detached from their resourcefulness when in the problem context. A lot of postgraduate study was dedicated to understanding how a neuro-linguistic programming (NLP) practitioner would operate in the coaching marketplace. The author found his professional development trajectory mirrored that of Grant, who says:

> Despite this disillusionment I remained interested in NLP. It seemed to hold much promise ... As my university psychological education progressed it become clear to me that many of the so-called NLP methodologies were long established in psychology and were 'NLP' in name and marketing only. (Grant 2019: 49)

Also in common with Grant, the author was not a great fan of mechanical rote-learned techniques which often follow from propositional knowledge. He preferred the new scholarship (Schön 1995), which flows from an action research perspective, meeting the everyday needs of people working in real-life situations and generated by an altogether different epistemology of knowledge by acquaintance and phenomenology (McNiff and Whitehead 2000).

However, in keeping with pluralist methodology this preference does not preclude a propositional and top-down approach. In coaching we primarily use language as our tool, and in reading the work of a former Associate Professor of Linguistics, Dr John Grinder, and later training with him, the author began to see the benefit of integrating the paradigm of transformational grammar (TG) into his work (Chomsky 1957). Specifically Grinder and Elgin (1973) say:

> It is this psychological closeness to one's native language, that prevents the individual from recognizing or noticing the intricacies and richness of that *system* ... The activity called linguistics will be the single most important activity in liberating one's head from the *structure* imposed by one's native language. (Grinder and Elgin 1973: 8; author's emphasis)

In addition to the CBC techniques mentioned above, the author began to house such techniques within a framework that paid attention to both systems thinking and structure. Maybe these splinter psyches or complexes identified by Jung were systemic and systematic psychological structures, composed of associated neuronal networks, operating according to Hebb's law (1949) and encoded in a way identified as the encoding specificity principle which states: 'the memory trace of an event and hence the properties of effective retrieval cues are determined by the specific encoding operations performed by the system on the input stimuli' (Tulving and Thomson 1973).

Just as language is hypothesized to have a structure and the lexicon and syntax implicitly encode our experience in a systemic and systematic way, maybe other aspects of our experience have structure too and these structures implicitly encode our way of experiencing similarly?

William James (1890), known as the father of psychology, noticed that we have three types of imagination – visual, auditory and motor – and in studying hypnosis recognized people store their memories in a timeline (Bolstad 2021). In attempting to understand the dilemma of determinism versus free will, and describing the brain as 'an instrument of possibilities, but of no certainties' (Hunt 2007: 176), James decided:

> I will assume for the present until next year that it is no illusion. My first act of free will shall be to believe in free will. I will go a step further with my will, not only act with it, but believe as well; believe in my individual reality. (Hunt 2007: 164)

James thus recognized that we act in the world, not on the basis of reality, but on the constructions of our mind-body system and the split-second decisions we make prior to their construction, development and maintenance. In adopting a pragmatic approach he did not suggest rather glibly that the truth is whatever works; rather he said if we compare the implications of the opposed solutions to a problem we can choose which one to believe in and act on.

So in a gestalt way, and through his own cycles of experience, in building the 7C's model, the author incorporated not only language and the assumptions of TG, but also other sensory structures and encouraged his clients occasionally to lose their mind and come to their senses in exploring the structure of their own subjective experience. In adopting this more phenomenological approach and using the client's personal experience as a data set, Tosey and Mathison discovered that the work of Grinder and his colleagues enhanced the precision and rigour of both explication interviews (the principal method used in psychophenomenology) and transcript analysis. Tosey and Mathison's paper specifically addressed the continual personal development area 'that is found in organizational practices such as executive coaching' (Tosey and Mathison 2010: 63).

Digging even deeper

In going even deeper and coaching on the edge where deep structures and even deeper structures need to be explored (Webb 2006), it is quite easy to understand why clients who have been derailed in their life agree to engage in a narrative which has at its centre propositions from a psychodynamic theoretical perspective. Some events of the past and the consequent internal psychological structures have not even made their way to conscious experience (primary gain). Also, within the coaching conversation it is discovered that as a result of these unconscious internal structures the coachee experiences certain additional gains (secondary gain). For example, a derailed executive who has thrived in the past due to an aggressive, competitive nature in a corporate culture which implicitly encouraged this attitude, may have to make fundamental changes in the way they now operate. Hypothetically this could require revisiting difficult times from their past, long forgotten and pushed down. Maybe they had been bullied or beaten, and in responding to this as creatively as they could, implicitly learned to bully others.

Maxwell (2009) makes a distinction between business/executive coaches who also have training in psychology and counselling, and those who do not. In her IPA study (interpretative phenomenological analysis) she demonstrated a tendency for the coaches with psychological and counselling training to work more at the boundary between the conscious and unconscious than those who do not have such training or the tools to deal effectively at this boundary.

The need for such tools and training for the modern coach is reinforced by recent findings in neuroscience. Using the reconsolidation of traumatic memories protocol (RTM) it has been discovered that in order to co-create new internal structures and reframe the old ones, the individual needs to re-experience in a minimal way the original events or series of events in order to render the internal structures labile and amenable to reframing. Early pharmacological studies indicate that reconsolidation depends on protein synthesis after a brief reminder of the target memory. The labile period begins about ten minutes after the reminder stimulus and lasts up to six hours (Gray and Bourke 2015).

Even though many may see this as the work of a psychotherapist, many coaches working with executives who have been derailed (Webb 2006) or who are corporate psychopaths (Babiak and Hare 2006) discover that developing techniques to work at this level is in fact very necessary in a coaching intervention. Mansi (2009), working with narcissists and using the Hogan Development Survey (HDS), discovered many dark triad characteristics of the narcissistic coachee. These included arrogance, inflated feelings of self-worth, disregard for others, charm, manipulativeness, risk-taking and impulsivity, to name just a few. She suggested to coaching psychologists that the key challenge in coaching the narcissist is how to reconcile two very important areas – a supreme sense of self-belief and the inability to reflect and see the need for any personal development.

Liston-Smith (2009) points out more than half of the 376 sample of coaches in Turner's (2010) award-winning research felt their coach training had inadequately prepared them to deal with unconscious processes. Liston-Smith says Turner's research suggests that it is not enough to say 'there's a line between coaching and therapy and you mustn't cross it'. Turner's research found that the unconscious is widely accepted as central in coaching. Most coaches perceived unconscious processes to be relevant to (89 per cent) and occur in (68 per cent) the majority of coaching conversations (N = 376). In dealing with these unconscious processes 7C's explicitly models the work of Rowan (1990) and Watkins and Watkins (1997), and works from the theoretical orientation of ego state psychology. This is particularly necessary in the modern coaching landscape – Graßmann and Schermuly (2017) found that when asked about difficulties in coaching per se, coaches still mentioned dark triad traits very frequently.

Figure 6.2 provides a visual of how 7C's represents these difficult and sometimes traumatic incidents from the past embedded in the internal psychological structure. Notice how when being coached in the context of 'Health' there is no negative interruption in the flow of experience by 'the Blues'. However, when being coached in the context of 'Career', a large area of negative blue emerges

Figure 6.2 7C's psychodynamic representation of a coaching client in two of seven differing contexts

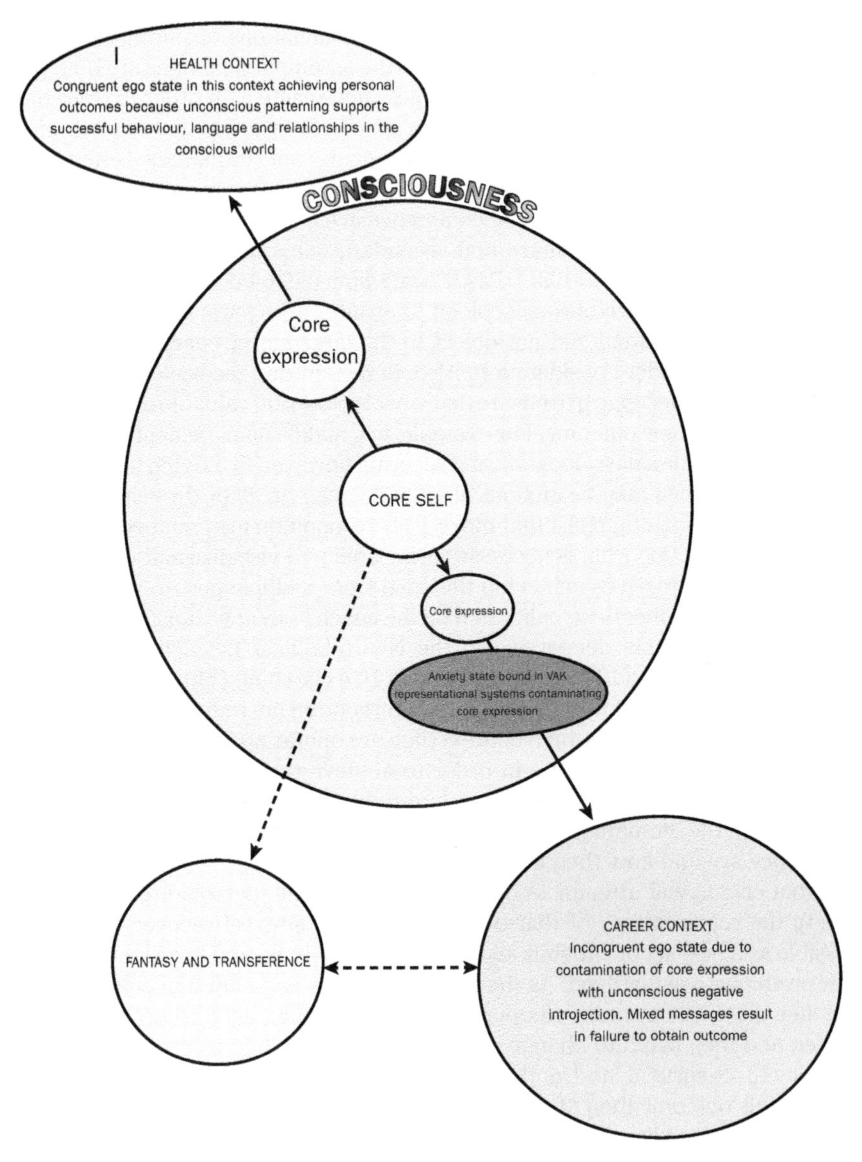

Source: Grimley (2020: 125).

which has previously interrupted the flow of experience in this context, and has been first introjected and then possibly assimilated by the client, providing mixed messages at the more conscious cognitive and behavioural levels (Grimley 2020: 124).

Pluralism and goal setting

Goal setting is one of the key elements in the foundations of pluralism. This is because implicit in the task of goal setting is the assumption humans are both purposeful and at cause, rather than meaningless and reactive. In order to overcome the resistance in clients mentioned above, a specific list was created of psychological variables which needed to be addressed so goals could be managed effectively. In 7C's, however, the term 'well-formed outcomes' (WFO) is used instead. This is because in order for the goal to be comprehensively addressed, the more unconscious elements such as primary and secondary gains need to be tackled. The author discovered Doran's (1981) SMART paradigm did not do this effectively, and so introduced such variables as ecology to ensure other parts of the coachee in other important contexts did not object to the direction of coaching within the specific context under consideration. Also, in recognizing the systemic nature of the psyche it was necessary to ensure that what is presently valuable to the coachee is retained in the new outcome. For example, in a middle management position the coachee may value salary, location and security, however, in moving upwards to a senior position they may be anxious about a decrease in all of these items in real terms and consequently resist that move. This recognition may not necessarily be a conscious one. Also what is necessary is the ability to visualize authentically the experience of themselves achieving this goal from multiple perceptual positions and to have this authenticity calibrated by the coach to mutual satisfaction.

To assist with this deeper work, the Neuro-Logical Level model of Dilts (1990), after Bateson (1972), is often used in 7C's coaching (Figure 6.3). What is found invariably is that in each coaching intervention not only does the coachee need to be fully aware of which context they are operating in, but they also need to know who they need to be in order to achieve their outcome comprehensively within that context and domain. Invariably that means understanding and researching the domain comprehensively to understand what the rules of excellence are and how they are specific to that context.

Often clients will attempt to operate from a default 'personality' in order to satisfy the requirements of that outcome in that context. However, this is not possible as a new set of capabilities often need to be built, and in order to do that, new strategies are involved. As the strategic level is negotiated in coaching, the coachee discovers in order to operationalize them they need to go deeper and higher, and they begin to change at the level of belief. In order to then become completely congruent and authentic in discharging who they need to be to achieve this outcome they often then find they need to revise some fundamental beliefs, and indeed literally at the level of identity begin to change who they are. The strapline of the Meta Program questionnaire called Alter Ego, that accompanies the 7C's model, is 'Be who you need to be to achieve what you value.'

Task switching

The psychology of task switching (Nass 2009; Charron and Koechlin 2010; Pea et al. 2012; Szumowska and Kossowska 2016, 2017) is therefore key in 7C's

Figure 6.3 Neurological levels

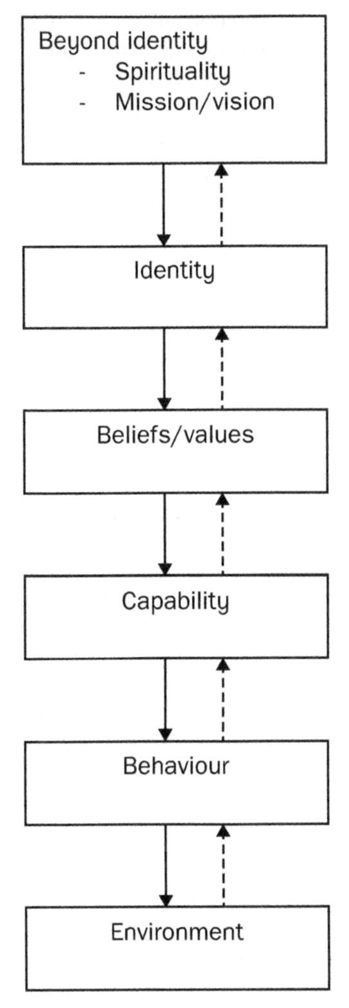

Adapted from Dilts (1990).

coaching, for it requires people to embrace their multiplicity and through time become familiar with a host of incredibly successful successive selves, fit for purpose in successive contexts (Radden 1996) which are automatically triggered in a variety of contexts throughout the day. For many this is an existential shift. However, given coaching is often regarded as taking people from the norm to an area of measurable excellence (Ericsson 2016), contrasted with counselling which is taking people from below the norm to the norm, this shift is regarded as necessary to fulfil the coaching psychological contract. When people are in the appropriate emotional state for one context in order to achieve one outcome, they often identify as somebody who is different compared with the person in another context who is achieving in a very different way and according to a different set of values and beliefs. However, as Rowan (1990) points out, these 'people' inhabit just one person. To attempt one outcome in one context with the inappropriate emotional state and identity is to court failure at the worst and achieve average performance at the best. In 7C's the way to discover what the appropriate emotional state and identity are, is achieved through behavioural modelling (Bandura 1977, 1986). Usually at the end of coaching the coachee literally feels like a brand new person. This managed dissociation is obviously very different from the chaotic and reactive dissociation of those suffering with dissociative identity disorder (DID), and the author continues with coachees to discover ways of switching between contexts that maximize authenticity, congruence, ownership and effectiveness and which are based on the most modern findings in the neuropsychology field. In keeping with the collaborative nature of pluralism, after one client called the people inside her 'Superheroes', this has been adopted by the author, with permission, going forwards.

A case study

Reginald is a world-class indoor rower officially ranked over many distances in the world in his age group. Initial contact was made by email on 11 December 2020 after filling in the 7C's Core Code questionnaire online, and a request was made for coaching to help him improve his mental fortitude in the context of sport. The first session was conducted on Thursday, 7 January 2021.

Reginald agreed to fill in Alter Ego as well and the results can be seen in Figures 6.4 and 6.5.

Alter Ego obtains an understanding for discussion of the Meta Programs a client possesses and Core Code, as described above, assesses levels of stress and how the coachee is dealing with the seven different contexts in their life. John Lilly (1967) regarded the human as analogous to a biocomputer and for him, at the higher neurological levels of Dilts (1990) sat what he called Metaprograms. These Metaprograms loosely can be referred generally to what psychologists call personality, and Lilly (1967: 180) believed that through 'self metaprogramming' people could change at this deeper level. For example, and in line with the work of Derks (2005), spatial proximity is known to moderate the amplification of shared experience (Boothby et al. 2016), and increasingly empirical research is showing that when in coaching we alter other perceptual variables such as time, direction, colour, weight, volume or size, the subjective experience changes too.

In this way 7C's adopts a very much more situational perspective towards coaching psychology (Mischel 1968, 1973). It recognizes that personality, rather than being an excuse for not being able to do something, is simply a neurological program. And that program can be co-revised/authored with the coachee to be something more useful, adopting a social learning paradigm, in keeping with

Figure 6.4 Alter Ego profile of Reginald along nine Meta Program dimensions (N = 814)

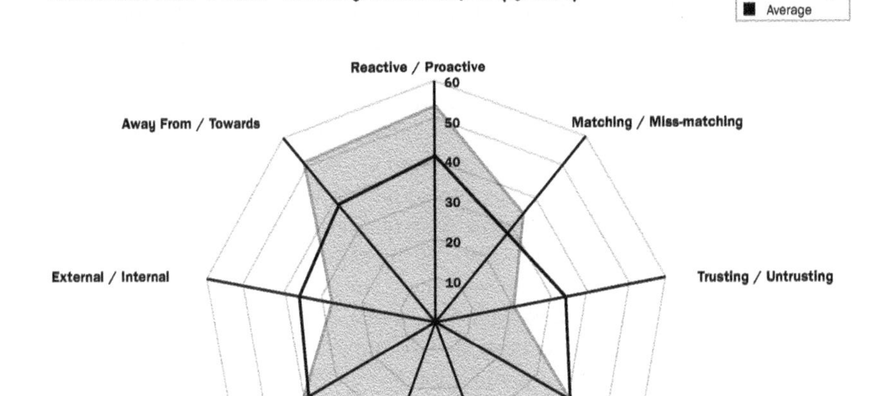

Figure 6.5 Core Code profile of Reginald compared with mean response (N = 271)

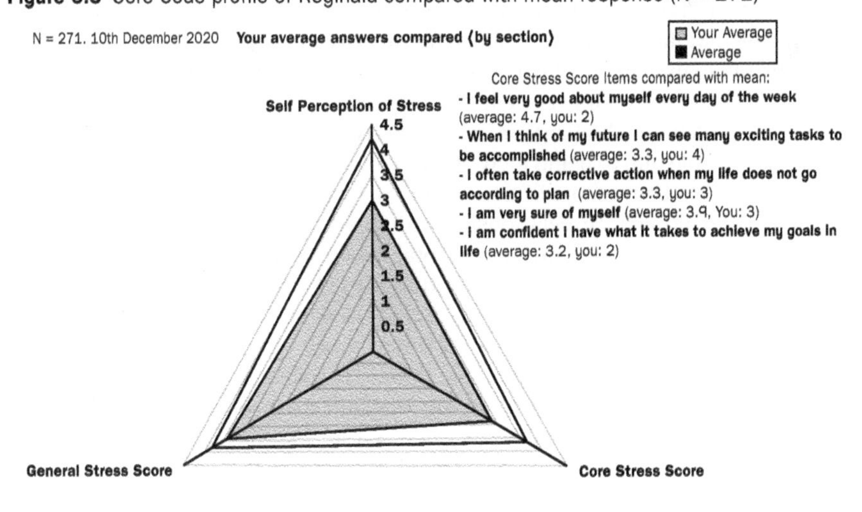

the modelling perspective of Bandura (1977, 1986), rather than the more stable and rigid trait models such as the well-known 5-factor model (Costa and McCrae 1994).

In discussing Alter Ego we recognized that, coming from a military background and working as a technical director for a major telecommunication company, Reginald had learned to be very structured in his approach and this was matched by the author in his coaching. The author set up training programmes to move Reginald from where he was to where he wished to be by the end of coaching. This was achieved by paying a great deal of attention to detail and having weekly correspondence to check the work being done and the feedback from the performances.

In one of the six coaching sessions we discussed how in the context of sport (which for Reginald fell into the 7C's context of Health), Reginald was a bit like his old Forces self with a lot of structure and attention to detail. However, this was not reflected in his Alter Ego profile which showed on both Options/Procedure and Small Chunk/Large Chunk dimensions he was returning corridor scores. Reginald explained that in the *context* of his sport he was very similar to when in the Forces, however, in his family life, where he was actually a big teddy bear, he was very Options-oriented. In responding to the Alter Ego questionnaire, for some of the items in those two dimensions he had imagined himself in differing contexts, thus the corridor scores.

One of the opportunities in coaching was to develop a persona specifically for Reginald's athletic outcomes, and in this case in the context of Health. As can be seen from the Core Code response set, Reginald fell well within the norms for experiencing stress, which indicated to the author he should be able to focus on the coaching appropriately. Reginald was blind in one eye, had torn cartilages which prevented him from running and for which he was scheduled for major surgery, and also had fractured his back in the past. Developing this persona (Superhero) was incredibly important for Reginald as he valued his health tremendously. He recognized that at his age he needed to take responsibility for ensuring he maintained his enthusiasm for health as he aged, rather than regressing to the mean in the UK, which he saw as overweight and unfit. In checking the ecology of the situation it was clear that, even though his workouts were incredibly intense and meant locking himself away from his children and wife and then being unavailable due to being incredibly exhausted, they were fully behind him. This was reflected by a score of 2 to item 13 in Core Code, which checks the context of intimate others: 'My relationship with those close to me is very good', with 1 being highest agreement and 8 being total disagreement.

In line with ego state psychology (Watkins and Watkins 1997) Reginald's new persona was named, and in this case called 'Reginald the Rock'. He spoke of clothing himself in this persona each time he sat down to row. Previous to coaching, even though Reginald had access to the strength of focus, attention, determination and ability to delete pain through the process of paying attention in a singular way to his WFO, he had not accessed this in the same way, compared with what 'Reginald the Rock' allowed in the context of rowing. Often he reported his mind wandering and sometimes psyching himself out of a hard session before it even started. Sometimes he would start a session and before it even got to the point of hurting, he would bail out as a result of intrusive thoughts of an unwanted nature, often from other contexts. Looking further at his Alter Ego profile it was noted that even though Reginald returned a very appropriate Proactive and Towards orientation, he was also very Externally referenced. In modelling other athletes he discovered that they tended to be very Internally referenced. They would seek out the expertise of others in coaching and specialist advice, but once they had gone through that process they became very internally referenced concerning their performance and what worked for them. Reginald noticed this was not so much the case for him, and he tended to continue to research ad infinitum, rather than come to a point of recognizing he was good enough now and he just needed to DO IT.

The key to making this coaching intervention very straightforward and simple was identifying precisely what the WFO was and recognizing that at that time there were characteristics within the coachee that did not support this WFO. Also key was continuing to ensure the ecology of the situation remained positive through repeat administrations of Core Code and finally the modelling of other top rowers and sportspeople, and assimilation of their perceived characteristics into Reginald the Rock. Finally, Reginald took ownership of these characteristics for himself and acquainted himself with the very special feel that textured his new co-constructed being whenever he sat down to row.

In requesting what it was precisely that made this coaching intervention work, Reginald's summary can be seen in Appendix 1.

Conclusion

This chapter looks at the eclectic nature of pluralist coaching and its assumptions, and has demonstrated how one coaching psychologist has developed over 25 years a particular pluralist methodology. This methodology and theoretical base continue to evolve as he learns from both his colleagues and his clients. Currently the author is continuing to build on the idea of the individual as a multiplicity, rather than a unity. This draws on the work of Jung, Watkins and Watkins, and Rowan and is embedded within transformational grammar, behavioural modelling and systems theory.

References

Babiak, P. and Hare, R.D. (2006) *Snakes in Suits: When Psychopaths Go to Work*. London: Harper.

Bandura, A. (1977) *Social Learning Theory*. Upper Saddle River, NJ: Prentice Hall.

Bandura, A. (1986) *The Social Foundations of Thought and Action*. Upper Saddle River, NJ: Prentice Hall.

Bateson, G. (1972) *Steps to an Ecology of Mind*. Chicago: University of Chicago Press.

Bolstad, R. (2021) William James: father of psychology, grandfather of NLP, Transformations website. Available at: https://transformations.org.nz/william-james/?fbclid=IwAR0J6GNSyAjEMLDizYUouD1XNMTAEwRPOOAK-mKejL7mEwIrUPvvTynipno (accessed 20 August 2021).

Boothby, E.J., Smith, L.K., Clark, M.S. and Bargh, J.A. (2016) Psychological distance moderates the amplification of shared experience, *Personality and Social Psychology Bulletin*, 42(10): 1431–44.

Charron, S. and Koechlin, E. (2010) Divided representation of concurrent goals in the human frontal lobes, *Science*, 328(5976): 360–3.

Chomsky, N. (1957) *Syntactic Structures*. The Hague: Mouton & Co.

Cooper, C.L. and Palmer, S. (2000) *Conquer Your Stress*. London: CIPD.

Cooper, M. and McLeod, J. (2007) A pluralistic framework for counselling and psychotherapy: Implications for research, *Counselling and Psychotherapy Research*, 7(3): 135–43.

Cooper, M. and McLeod, J. (2010) Pluralism: Towards a new paradigm for therapy, *Therapy Today*, November. Available at: https://www.researchgate.net/publication/279534378 (accessed 25 August 2021).

Costa, P.T. and McCrae, R.R. (1994) Set like plaster? Evidence for the stability of adult personality, in T.F. Heatherton and J.L. Weinbergr (eds) *Can Personality Change?* Washington, DC: American Psychological Association, pp. 21–40.

Csikszentmihalyi, M. (1990) *Flow: The Psychology of Optimal Experience*. New York: HarperCollins.

Derks, L.A.C. (2005) *Social Panoramas: Changing the Unconscious Landscape with NLP and Psychotherapy*. Carmarthen: Crown House.

Dilts, R. (1990) *Changing Belief Systems with NLP*. Capitola, CA: Meta Publications.

Doran, G.T. (1981) There's a SMART way to write management's goals and objectives, *Management Review*, 70(11): 35–6.

Downing, J.N. (2004) Psychotherapy practice in a pluralistic world: Philosophical and moral dilemmas, *Journal of Psychotherapy Integration*, 14(2): 123–48.

Ericsson, A. (2016) *Peak: Secrets from the New Science of Expertise*. New York: Houghton Mifflin Harcourt.

Grant, A.M. (2019) A personal perspective on neuro-linguistic programming: Reflecting on the tension between personal experience and evidence-based practice, *International Coaching Psychology Review*, 14(1): 45–56.

Graßmann, C. and Schermuly, C.C. (2017) The role of neuroticism and supervision in the relationship between negative effects for clients and novice coaches, *Coaching: An International Journal of Theory, Research and Practice*, 11(1): 74–88.

Gray, R. and Bourke, F. (2015) *Remediation of Intrusive Symptoms of PTSD in Fewer than Five Sessions: A 30-Person Pre-Pilot Study of the RTM Protocol*. Corning, NY: The Research and Recognition Project.

Grimley, B. (2002) Sexy variables, *Rapport Journal*, Summer.

Grimley, B. (2005) Sailing the 7 C's of courage, *AC Bulletin*, Summer.

Grimley, B. (2013) *Theory and Practice of NLP Coaching: A Psychological Approach*. London: Sage.

Grimley, B. (2015) What is NLP? Doctoral thesis, University of Central Nicaragua (UCN). Available at: http://ow.ly/XQqcA (accessed 9 October 2018).

Grimley, B. (2016) What is NLP? The development of a grounded theory of neuro-linguistic programming (NLP), within an action research journey: Implications for the use of NLP in coaching psychology, *International Coaching Psychology Review*, 11(2): 166–78.

Grimley, B. (2019) The need for neuro-linguistic programming to develop greater construct validity, *International Coaching Psychology Review*, 14(1): 31–44.

Grimley, B. (2020) *The 7C's of Coaching: A Personal Journey Through the World of NLP and Coaching Psychology*. New York: Routledge.

Grimley, B. (2021a) Sailing the 7C's of courage. A framework for one-to-one work emerging from neuro-linguistic programming (NLP) – a single case history, *Journal of Experiential Psychotherapy*, 24(1(93)): 3–17.

Grimley, B. (2021b) Sailing the 7C's of Courage – away from the practice of NLP and towards a novel and cohesive theory of change. A single case history, *Journal of Experiential Psychotherapy*, 24(2(94)): 3–11.
Grinder, J. and Elgin, S.H. (1973) *Guide to Transformational Grammar: History, Theory, Practice*. New York: Holt, Rinehart and Winston.
Hebb, D.O. (1949) *The Organization of Behavior: A Neuropsychological Theory*. New York: John Wiley & Sons.
Hollanders, H. (2000) Eclecticism/integration: Historical developments, in S. Palmer and R. Woolfe (eds) *Integrative and Eclectic Counselling and Psychotherapy*. London: Sage, pp. 1–30.
Hunt, M.H. (2007) *The Story of Psychology*. New York: Anchor Books (Kindle edition).
James, W. (1890) *The Principles of Psychology*, 2 vols. New York: Henry Holt.
James, W. (1996) *A Pluralistic Universe*. Lincoln, NE: University of Nebraska Press.
Lilly, J.C. (1967) *Programming the Human Biocomputer*. Oakland, CA: Ronin Publishing.
Liston-Smith, J. (2009) SGCP conference report highlighting the psychology in coaching. 1st European Coaching Psychology Conference, 17–18 December 2008, *The Coaching Psychologist*, 5(1): 45–52.
Mansi, A. (2009) Coaching the narcissist: How difficult can it be? Challenges for coaching psychologists, *The Coaching Psychologist*, 5(1): 22–5.
Maxwell, A. (2009) How do business coaches experience the boundary between coaching and therapy/counselling?, *Coaching: An International Journal of Theory, Research and Practice*, 2(2): 149–62.
McLennan, G. (1995) *Pluralism*. Buckingham: Open University Press.
McNiff, J. and Whitehead, J. (2000) *Action Research in Organisations*. London: Routledge.
Miller, S.D., Duncan, B.L. and Hubble, M.A. (1997) Escape from Babel: Toward a unifying language for psychotherapy practice. New York: WW Norton. In Thomas, M.L. (2006) The contributing factors of change in a therapeutic process, *Contemporary Family Therapy*, 28(2): 201–10. doi: 10.1007/s10591-006-9000–4.
Mischel, W. (1968) *Personality and Assessment*. New York: Wiley.
Mischel, W. (1973) Toward a cognitive social learning reconceptualization of personality, *Psychological Review*, 80(4): 252–83.
Nass, C. (2009) Multitasking may not mean higher productivity, NPR website. Available at: https://www.npr.org/templates/story/story.php?storyId=112334449&ft=1&f=5 (accessed 29 August 2021).
Norcross, J.C. (2005) A primer on psychotherapy integration, in J.C. Norcross and M.R. Goldfried (eds) *Handbook of Psychotherapy Integration*. New York: Oxford University Press, pp. 3–23.
Paul, G.L. (1969) Behavior modification research: Design and tactics, in C.M. Franks (ed.) *Behavior Therapy Appraisal and Status*. New York: McGraw-Hill, pp. 29–62.
Pea, R., Nass, C., Meheula, L. et al. (2012) Media use, face-to-face communication, media multitasking, and social well-being among 8- to 12-year-old girls, *Developmental Psychology*, 48(2): 327–36.
Pendle, A. (2015) Pluralistic coaching? An exploration of the potential for a pluralistic approach to coaching, *International Journal of Evidence Based Coaching and Mentoring*, Special Issue 9, June: 1–13.
Radden, J. (1996) *Divided Minds and Successive Selves: Ethical Issues in Disorders of Identity and Personality*. Cambridge, MA: Massachusetts Institute of Technology.
Rescher, N. (1993) *Pluralism: Against the Demand for Consensus*. Oxford: Oxford University Press.

Rowan, J. (1990) *Subpersonalities: The People Inside Us*. London: Routledge.
Samuels, A. (1985) *Jung and the Post-Jungians*. London: Routledge.
Schön, D.A. (1995) The new scholarship requires a new epistemology, *Change*, 27(6): 26–34.
Szumowska, E. and Kossowska, M. (2016) Need for closure and multitasking performance: The role of shifting ability, *Personality and Individual Differences*, 96: 12–17.
Szumowska, E. and Kossowska, M. (2017) Motivational rigidity enhances multitasking performance: The role of handling interruptions, *Personality and Individual Differences*, 106: 81–9.
Tosey, P. and Mathison, J. (2010) Exploring inner landscapes through psychophenomenology. The contribution of neuro-linguistic programming to innovations in researching first person experience, *Qualitative Research in Organizations and Management: An International Journal*, 5(1): 63–82.
Tulving, E. and Thomson, D.M. (1973) Encoding specificity and retrieval processes in episodic memory, *Psychological Review*, 80(5): 352–73.
Turner, E. (2010) Coaches' views on the relevance of unconscious dynamics to executive coaching, *Coaching: An International Journal of Theory, Research and Practice*, 3(1): 12–29.
Wampold, B. (2001) *The Great Psychotherapy Debate: Models, Methods and Findings*. Mahwah, NJ: Erlbaum.
Watkins, J.G. and Watkins, H.H. (1997) *Ego States, Theory and Therapy*. New York: WW Norton.
Webb, P.J. (2006) Back on track: The coaching journey in executive career derailment, *International Coaching Psychology Review*, 1(2): 68–74.

Appendix 1

Summary of Coaching by 'Reginald'

Where I believed I was the limiting factor, you enabled me to pull on resources I never knew existed within me. You seeded and created the environment for Reginald the Rock to grow and we reaped the benefits from this. What really helped was your enthusiasm and belief in me. You pointed out if others could do it, so could I and, by paying attention to the detail of my initial mind-set, recognized I was not using my resources effectively. The modelling projects and consistent use of pictures of top athletes performing at international events helped me understand how important physiology is to performance and how initially my mind kept wandering. Your persistent belief in me and re-structuring of key workouts that really stretched me, helped me to develop 'Reginald the Rock'. The recognition that this person had a job to do, gave him permission to be so much more focused on the job at hand. My focus now is so much better and also means when my work out is done, I am able to attend with 100 per cent attention to other contexts in my life, knowing that during my time on the rower I have given everything and not held anything back. My improvement in performance and rankings speak for themselves. Thank you so much.

(Personal correspondence)

7 Psychology disciplines informing coaching psychology practice

Manfusa Shams

Summary

The distinctive approach of coaching psychology practice indicates that coaching psychology is an applied discipline with a practice-focused developmental approach to serve non-clinical population groups.

The chapter presents the interdisciplinary contribution to developing coaching psychology practice, as well as the influence of the different subject-specific knowledge on differential coaching practice. The discussion highlights the need for cross-disciplinary fertilization and interdisciplinary collaboration to develop and share knowledge in coaching psychology and coaching psychology practice.

Keywords: coaching psychology practice, coaching outcomes, coaching and education, sports coaching, health coaching, business coaching.

Introduction

Coaching psychology is informed by different areas of psychology and coaching psychology practice is also influencing other areas of psychology in practice. This chapter presents the dominant influence of coaching psychology practice in a few selected areas. Coaching psychology is built on the interdisciplinary knowledge base, and as such many coaching practices are designed and developed using the subject knowledge in these areas. Coaching practice is essentially a practice for development of individuals in various settings, hence we can expect mutually exclusive interdisciplinary approaches in coaching practice.

Aims

This chapter aims to present evidence-based discussion of a few selected psychology specialisms informing coaching psychology practice, and the application of coaching psychology to different areas, such as education and health.

The discussion demonstrates how coaching psychology practice can be applied to different subject areas.

Coaching psychology practice: an interdisciplinary perspective

The core elements in coaching psychology are application and practice. These elements are found in all subject areas, implying that coaching psychology practice has a wide application, if and when appropriate tools, techniques and approaches are developed, justified and verified. In this chapter I have discussed the dominant influence of coaching psychology practice in a few selected specialist subject areas to offer further thoughts and discussion on the interdisciplinary approach in coaching psychology practice. The critical issue is to identify the approaches specific to coaching psychology, and to support individuals to gain personal development, goal attainment and self-fulfilment using relevant interdisciplinary subject-specific knowledge.

Coaching psychology practice can serve all areas of human development using relevant coaching approaches, tools and techniques. However, the coaching needs for individuals are mainly predominant in education, work, health and sports, and the discussion in this chapter is focused in these areas. The discussion has drawn relevant theories and research evidence to elucidate the significant positive impact of coaching psychology on supporting individuals to reach the optimum level of functioning in these areas.

Coaching psychology in education

The use of coaching in education has a long history since the assumed teacher-coach role during 1906–16 (Lewis 1969). However, coaching at this time was mainly an instructional role performance and specific to a particular sport, such as football. Coaching in this context lacked any systematic use of psychological knowledge in coaching practice. Hence, coaching during the 1900s was mainly an instructor and guidance role, and limited to soliciting advice to follow instructions, and consultancy (Kilburg 2016).

Coaching practice in the educational sector did not become prevalent until the late 1970s. Then this was mainly limited to serving as a coach for physical education programmes. For example, a physical education teacher had a dual role in practice, using a teacher-coach model in a school. The tension of switching this role from a teacher to a coach and vice versa was complex and less productive (Locke and Massengale 1978; Sage 1987). Hence a more refined approach was drawn up later in the 1980s to separate the coach role from the teacher's role, with the aim of serving each role efficiently (Figone 1994). This initiative in the higher education sector was instrumental in drawing the attention of policymakers and legislative authorities – for example, with formal decisions from different sectors to endorse and include coaching psychology in various educational sectors and professional practice from the 1990s, and most recently widely accepted positive effects of coaching interventions for schools and the NHS in the UK (NHS 2021). There has been a sharp rise in accepting coaching psychology practice to influence education practice in the UK. For example, a dedicated site has been created as a guide for schools planning to develop coaching practice to improve teaching and learning (Lofthouse et al. 2010).

The popularity of coaching in the educational sector has facilitated the progress of coaching psychology practice to improve learning and learners' well-being (van Nieuwerburgh and Knight 2019). The practice of coaching using psychological theories and research has been applied to various areas of education, for example, primary and secondary schools, health professionals, distance learning, peer-assisted learning and leadership education (Wood et al. 2016; Matthewman et al. 2018).

The application of coaching psychology is not limited to practice, but also extended to evidence-based research and developing educational policies. Using a narrative qualitative research method, Macleod (2018) found significant positive changes in the leadership behaviour of women in academic leadership positions after a coaching intervention. These included increased mindfulness and presence, self-awareness and confidence, and action-oriented decision-making leading to transformative change. The impact of coaching on educational performance has been a hot topic in recent times, especially due to the rapid changes in the educational environment as traditional classroom teaching is replaced with virtual learning platforms using advanced innovative educational technology and virtual tools. This technology-aided virtual educational platform is meeting the growing need for distance learning in different parts of a country, and also serving the global community using one educational platform. It is interesting that academic coaching is effective in increasing retention rates for distance learning students (Vadell 2017). This finding has confirmed that coaching interventions underpinned by psychological theories and research evidence have far-reaching effects on educational performance irrespective of the mode of delivery and delivery techniques.

The question is why coaching intervention is useful for behavioural performance and changes in an educational context. Here we are emphasizing behavioural performance as behavioural outcomes from coaching, and giving less attention to the neurological and cognitive functions as a result of coaching (Shams 2015). The positive effect of coaching and the effect size, expected behavioural outcomes and outcome levels in an educational context are summarized in Table 7.1.

The 'effect' in Table 7.1 represents responses to coaching interventions and 'outcome' refers to changes from the coaching intervention. The effect size of coaching psychology practice in education on cognitive enhancement and behavioural or performance-related changes can be high or low, and this influences

Table 7.1 Effects and behavioural outcomes: coaching psychology practice in education

Effects	Effect size	Effect levels	Outcome size	Outcome levels	Challenging issues
Cognitive enhancement	High-low	Advanced-elementary	High/low	Less/no change/ full transformation	Measurement
Behavioural/ performance changes	High-low	Advanced-elementary	High/low	Less/no change/ full transformation	Measurement
Mutually exclusive	High-high Low-low High-low Low-high	Combination	Combination	Combination	Measurement
					Sustainability
					Reflection

the effect level, and outcome size and levels. For example, the effect size of a coaching intervention on cognitive enhancement might be low but behavioural changes might be high, so the effect level may remain at the elementary level for cognitive enhancement but rise to advanced level for behavioural changes. In relation to outcome size and levels, this could be low with no change for cognitive, with high and full transformation for behavioural performance.

Coaching intervention effect size and levels can also be mutually exclusive in making an impact on cognitive functioning and behavioural change. Thus this can be both high and low for cognitive and behavioural, and the outcome can also be a combination of high-high or low-low. An example might be school students' performance assessment on a continuous basis to find out the coaching intervention effect size and levels. An end-of-year assessment can be used to explore the size and levels of coaching outcomes. The mutually exclusive effect and outcome size and levels can be ascertained using both cognitive and behavioural measures during the academic sessions and at the end of the academic year.

The critical issues here are related to the measurement of coaching effects and outcomes, i.e. how can we measure the effect size and levels, or outcome size and levels of coaching intervention? These issues can be addressed using either a simple or a complex approach. To follow a simple approach, a coaching practitioner can use existing tools and techniques. Or it can be more complex if a holistic and inclusive approach is considered, in which cognitive and behavioural effects and outcomes are separated out using relevant techniques and measurements to assess their relative position as a result of coaching interventions. This will help to trace the intensity and depth of the coaching intervention for making changes in an individual's cognitive and behavioural domains. The other two challenging issues are sustainability and reflection, which represent the sustainable effect size and levels, as well as sustainable outcome size and levels. The reflective element in coaching intervention, both for the coach and coachee, is likely to influence the sustainable outcomes and levels.

The application of this framework in an educational context may support the inherent value of coaching intervention for learners and teachers, education and training providers, researchers and consultants.

Chapter 4 sets out a proposed 'selective realism' conceptual model for practitioners, highlighting the underlying psychological properties of coaching intervention that can provide an inclusive and holistic developmental coaching approach to raise awareness of selected issues (selective realism) affecting individuals' development and progression. This includes neurological, behavioural and cognitive elements operating simultaneously during the coaching intervention. The interactive elements can remain active until the end of a formal coaching intervention to facilitate the process of achieving an optimum level of coaching outcomes. The developmental approach in the coaching process thus has an enabling element to support the expected changes in an individual's neurological, cognitive and behavioural outcomes.

In an educational context, a coaching intervention aided by an inclusive and holistic approach has enormous effect on the performance of the learners as it takes account of the cognitive and behavioural aspects of the learners. The neurological progression is embedded in the developmental change, and can be traced, measured and identified using relevant modern tools and techniques such as fMRI and MRI. Coaching intervention underpinned by psychological knowledge has immense educational value, for example, intellectual growth through enhanced cognitive development, neurological changes and demonstrable behavioural responses to the learning needs.

We can expect coaching psychology practice to flourish in all educational contexts and across all nations due to the powerful learning elements inherent in coaching practice to bring about changes in individuals' development.

Occupational/work psychology informing coaching psychology practice

Coaching psychology is successfully delivering coaching interventions to address various issues affecting individuals' performance, well-being and goal attainment in diverse work contexts. The most widely used areas of coaching in an organization and work context are leadership coaching and team coaching. This section presents how coaching psychology can be applied to advance and develop organizational behaviour, accelerating occupational performance and occupational health. The aim is to highlight the value of coaching psychology as an applied and solution-focused approach to many issues in an organizational work context for improving individuals' work behaviour and performance, well-being, and personal and professional development. Coaching psychology practice provides a bridge over the interdisciplinary knowledge transfer and professional skills development platform. The following section presents the influence of occupational psychology in coaching practice.

Psychology in coaching: occupational/work context

Occupational psychology facilitates change to achieve improved work performance and working environment (Millward 2005). The meeting point of occupational and coaching psychology is the 'facilitator's role for making a change'. The driving force from each discipline is focused on improving performance at a maximum level, which is referred to as the 'peak performance and optimum level of performance' in coaching psychology. But what is the difference between these two discipline-based practices? This leads us to the fundamental question, whether there is any hard distinctive line between any sub-disciplines of psychology, as they are all grounded on the main, or basic, psychological principles. The question can be addressed using an analogy of farmland in which crops are cultivated to gain the maximum yield from the land. However, if the crops do not grow well, then the land will not be able to return the expected yield. Here the farm is an organization and the practice of occupational psychology is focused on improving the quality of the land to change the production quality and amount of crops grown. The performance of the crops can be regarded as under the remit of coaching psychology. A coaching intervention will involve applying different solutions to change, improve and maintain the quality and production of crops. The interdependency of the land and crops indicates the value of two different disciplinary approaches to gain the maximum benefit for an individual – the farmer in this case – and the farm as an organization.

A coaching intervention to support a coachee in an organizational context is expected to benefit both the employee/coachee and the employer/organization. The main difference between occupational and coaching practice in this context is that in coaching psychology the driver of the change is the individual/coachee themselves, whereas occupational psychology practice is driven by the occupational psychology practitioners, who execute their plan to address occupational challenges – such as developing recruitment and training policies, evaluating existing practices to improve performance, or a communication and leadership strategy using a focused approach to make changes in the organization as a whole (Evans and Warren 2019). Coaching psychology practice is a partnership between the coach and the coachee in which mutual trust and understanding play a major role in achieving successful coaching outcomes. Occupational psychology practice is a directive practice with the leading role taken by an occupational psychology practitioner. Coaching psychology intervention is provided at a micro level (individuals and small group/team), whereas occupational psychology practice is focused mainly on the macro level (organization). This is the major difference between these two disciplinary approaches to

Table 7.2 Disciplinary approach, application and practice outcomes in coaching and occupational psychology practice

Disciplinary approach	Application	Practice outcomes
Coaching psychology practice	Psychological knowledge specific to supporting/ developing an individual	Individual and group personal development/behavioural change and goal attainment
Occupational psychology practice	Psychological knowledge specific to work behaviour and organizational culture	Development and enhancement of organizational behaviour/ functioning
Combined/interactive	Coaching intervention to employees and occupational intervention to organization simultaneously	Individual and organizational changes, and sustainable progress to attain both personal and organizational goals
General psychological issues	Supporting individuals and organizations	Sustainable change and progressive development

achieve effective practice outcomes (Boysen-Rotelli 2020). Table 7.2 above summarizes the key features of occupational and coaching psychology practices.

The exclusive practice of coaching psychology in an organizational context was not fully established until the nineteenth century, although leadership consultancy began from the Second World War. The interesting developments of executive and leadership coaching came from within the consultancy domain. During the 1980s many consulting companies started to acknowledge the influence of coaching on leadership development, independent of consulting practice (Thompson 1987; Kilburg 1996). However, this was not actually leadership coaching as it has been used in more recent times (Kilburg 2007).

The following section provides a critical summary of leadership and executive coaching to highlight how coaching psychology is influencing issues relating to leadership behaviour, and how knowledge about this area of work/ occupational psychology is developing leadership coaching.

Leadership and executive coaching

The most popular and effective coaching intervention for supporting individuals in a work context is leadership and executive coaching. Despite using various methods and techniques, the consistency in obtaining positive effects from coaching intervention for changes in the expected direction of leadership behaviour and executive behaviour is very promising.

The key question is, what are the underlying psychological constructs facilitating effective leadership coaching? This question can be addressed in relation to motivational factors, personality types and relevant situational factors. The major psychological construct underpinning leadership coaching is 'the psychology of facilitation and development' in relation to a specific set of activities designed for a leader to execute. A coaching intervention facilitates the leader's efforts to develop their role functions to achieve the expected behavioural outcome, and to meet the organizational demands (Shams 2022). This is accomplished using relevant psychometric tools, measures, and relevant coaching techniques and approaches. This implies that development is the central feature of leadership coaching (Sperry 2013). An example of an effective coaching intervention for leadership is the application of 360-degree assessment of leadership behaviour. This measure, which is often referred to as 'multirater assessment', focuses on evaluating leadership behaviours from different sources, thereby providing a 360-degree view of the behaviour under a coaching lens. Examples of other applications are psychometric tests to assess skills and competencies, personality and team-building skills.

Leadership coaching has raised many interesting and critical issues for business teams and various functional teams in an organizational context. This has generated the groundwork for team coaching intervention using the psychology of team behaviour. Team coaching intervention is one of the most popular coaching interventions for organizational change, which may or may not be applied in conjunction with leadership coaching (Shams 2022). Team coaching alongside one-to-one leadership coaching is thought to be the most effective intervention for making changes in the organizational culture as well as leaders' and employees' behaviour. Leadership coaching is embedded within an organizational context, and business coaching often includes leadership coaching in the intervention stages.

Business coaching

The most widely used coaching intervention is called business coaching. However, the groundwork for business coaching using psychological knowledge was not clearly established until quite recently (Boysen-Rotelli 2020). A business coaching approach aims to optimize work-related behaviour in a business setting (Theeboom et al. 2014). Its primary focus is improving business functions using accelerated employee performance through coaching intervention. A coaching intervention looks into the business/organizational culture, employer–employee relations and communications, employees' performance behaviour etc., within the organizational context. This multiple approach in coaching intervention often leads to applying coaching to a leader in the business, and team coaching simultaneously (Shams 2022). Business coaching thus includes multiple approaches to support organizational development, and it is now regarded as an important employer's tool to improve business functions (Boysen-Rotelli 2020). Coachee engagement and reflective understanding of the need to improve personal and professional skills for business growth in an organizational context can bring the effective desired changes in the organizational culture and performance.

Business coaching is diversified, using different approaches, tools and techniques. There are also different types of business coaching using different models, e.g. solution-focused, cognitive behavioural and gestalt approaches (Spoth et al. 2013), family system theory (Shams 2022), and the existential approach (Spinelli and Horner 2018). Coaching psychology practice supports the performance of teams, employees and leaders, and as such the practice is useful for the organization as a whole.

Coaching psychology is a new discipline, hence there is a lot of developmental work to be completed. This includes documenting contributions from coaching psychology to different areas of psychology, and continuing research to strengthen interdisciplinary approaches in coaching psychology practice.

Coaching psychology practice and health psychology

There is increasing interest in applying coaching psychology practice to address the health and well-being of an individual, which is related to changing health behaviour using relevant coaching tools. The application of coaching psychology to health and well-being is different to health psychology practice: for example, health psychology is primarily focused on examining the underlying biological, psychosocial and environmental factors affecting an individual's health and illness. The change agent here is the individual, and as such this is similar to a coaching psychology intervention for changing health behaviour. However, coaching psychology is not focused on health and illness issues, but rather on supporting an individual to change their behaviour to achieve their fully functioning self, using mechanisms such as strengthening and commitment, awareness and resilience etc. Coaching psychology application is directed towards achieving human functioning at an optimum level and considers individuals' perception of, and attitudes towards, their developmental needs. Health psychology, on the other hand, is focused on managing individuals' positive health outcomes using a biopsychosocial model, and the practice is usually delivered to clinical populations with physical health symptoms. Health psychologists work with multi-agency health professionals to bring changes in the health and health behaviour of clinically vulnerable individuals or groups. This has been one of the most successful psychological interventions for alleviating health and illness problems since the beginning of the nineteenth century. Coaching psychology is a relatively new psychology specialist area with a developmental focus on non-clinical populations. The driving force in a change context is individuals themselves, and a coaching practitioner is merely present in the transformational process during coaching sessions. Coaching psychology is expected to proliferate in the coming years with increasing practice, research and publications.

A critical analysis of coaching psychology application to change and improve health behaviour provides the following essential features, as presented in Table 7.3. A coaching practice driven by relevant theories and models can bring behavioural change at an individual level, and lifestyle change at a national level.

Table 7.3 Key features of health coaching intervention

Coaching psychology	Practice	Application	Outcome
Health coaching	Theory, model	Coaching intervention	Development and change
	Change, maintain	Coaching intervention	Transformation
Individualized	Individual coaching	Coaching intervention	Behavioural change, improvement
National	Mass level/group coaching	NHS and others globally	Lifestyle change

Coaching psychology intervention is increasingly valued and recognized in the health sectors. For example, the UK National Health Service (NHS) has now introduced a leadership coaching programme (NHS 2021). The principal feature of coaching psychology practice in the health context is the application of relevant psychological theories and models to make changes and maintain those changes in the lifestyles of individuals and groups. For example, the most frequently cited theoretical models are self-determination theory, the trans-theoretical model of change, motivational interviewing, the cycle of change for health behaviour and social cognitive theory. The focus is on supporting individuals to achieve their desired health outcomes. Health coaching is thus regarded as an intervention tool for developing personal abilities, capacities and skills to make positive changes in behaviour (Lee et al. 2021). Research evidence supports the application of self-determination theory in coaching practice to change, improve and maintain motivation and self-determination in relation to health behaviour.

The application of relevant psychological theories and models is varied and dependent on the different types of health coaching. For example, Sforzo et al. (2019) discussed the positive effects of health coaching on weight loss and obesity, diabetes, heart disease, hypertension, cancer and cholesterol management. The positive effect is related to changes in lifestyles and behavioural changes linked to improving personal well-being. This warrants a word of caution about not drawing the misleading conclusion that health coaching can alleviate physical illness directly; the impact of health coaching is indirect, for example, bringing about behavioural changes related to the lifestyles of individuals. From this perspective, coaching psychology practice for health behaviour is distinctively different to health psychology practice.

Health psychology practice aims to understand the underlying psychosocial factors affecting the health conditions described above in order to support the health care system to address the influence of these factors on the onset and prognosis of physical and health-related illness. It is thus often integrated into the broad health care system, and health psychologists work in the health and social care sectors. Unlike coaching psychology practice, the target population for health psychology practice is clinical and health-risk individuals and groups. Coaching psychology practice in a health context, often called 'health coaching', is not yet an accredited form of training, and lacks systematic regulation to ensure that a scientific, evidence-based coaching intervention is delivered to improve and maintain healthy lifestyles and health behaviours. However, promising development has been made in the United States to integrate health coaching into the health care system, recognizing the positive effects of health coaching on health behaviours (Moore 2021). It is expected that this initiative will encourage coaching psychology practice to be institutionalized across the globe.

Coaching psychology influencing sports psychology practice

Coaching in sports has a long established history. Coaching has been in practice since Ancient Greece – mainly focused on training wrestlers and archers (Robinson 2010). Coaching practice at that time involved directive instruction using strict rules and regulations, including reprimands for failure to achieve the expected standard. Coaching practice during the fifth and sixth centuries BC was similar to any physical training. Rather than providing a personalized supportive coaching approach, early sports coaching was a force to drive an individual to excel in physical performance, disregarding the psychosocial factors affecting their performance quality and level, and their physical capacity to attain the target set by the coach/trainer. The use of the term 'coaching' at that time was misleading, and the practice was mainly a physical training route guided by political gains (wrestling was used as a part of winning conflicts/in war zone areas).

The emergence of coaching psychology has helped to separate conventional sports coaching practice from coaching psychology practice for sports, using evidence-based practice, empirical research and professional regulation. Conventional sports coaching is still in practice, predominantly in the context of health and fitness. However, this is focused mainly on training, guidance and mentoring. Coaching psychology practice for sports has applied the core principles of coaching psychology to develop individuals to reach their optimum level of physical and mental functioning in the sports sector. These principles include consideration of the complex social environment, organizational structure and psychological factors affecting performance in sports (Cropley et al. 2020). A sports coaching practitioner supports the process of developing athletes and teams to improve and maintain individual performance in sports, including effective team functions to excel in performance to reach the desired goal of the team. Sports coaching intervention is hence quite commonly applied to individuals separately and as a group or team. This can be a complex intervention process in terms of delivering individual and team coaching separately or simultaneously.

The special feature of sports coaching is a focused approach to improve and maintain the health and well-being of individuals engaged in sports and sports-related activities. Recent research is increasingly warning against a singular coaching intervention approach in which sports performers are the main focus, which can lead to ineffective coaching outcomes (McCarthy and Giges 2017). This is because sports coaching practitioners are constantly judged by their performance in achieving successful sports outcomes, disregarding sports performers' own individual factors. Sports coaching practice using sports psychology principles considers multiple factors affecting coaching outcomes, including sports, organizational structure, developmental strategy and organizational goals. Figure 7.1 shows the complexity of the practice of sports coaching and a possible solution-focused approach to untangle the complexity. The detailed description of each part of Figure 7.1 is presented in Table 7.4.

The major feature of sports psychology coaching is that it is focused on changing the performance of individuals engaged in sports and sports activities. Hence, a coaching psychologist must have specialist knowledge in sports psychology, which includes understanding of the sport's organizational culture, sports team coaching and interprofessional collaboration (sports management, sports delivery, etc.). In addition, understanding of critical issues affecting the performance of a coachee is important. These include personal and professional developmental needs, sports, organizational structure and performance, commitment and engagement in the coaching process, coaching outcome delivery and implementation, and evaluation of the coaching intervention with the aim to support performance enhancement and maintenance. Similar to any coaching intervention, the interactive critical factors are mutual understanding and trust, intention and motivation to change, perceived coaching environment and organizational constraints.

Sports coaching using sports psychology principles predominantly applies a solution-focused approach to address the coaching needs. This approach seems to correspond to the fundamentals of coaching psychology practice in terms of supporting a coachee to harness their existing resources to change and improve

Figure 7.1 Complex web of sports coaching psychology practice

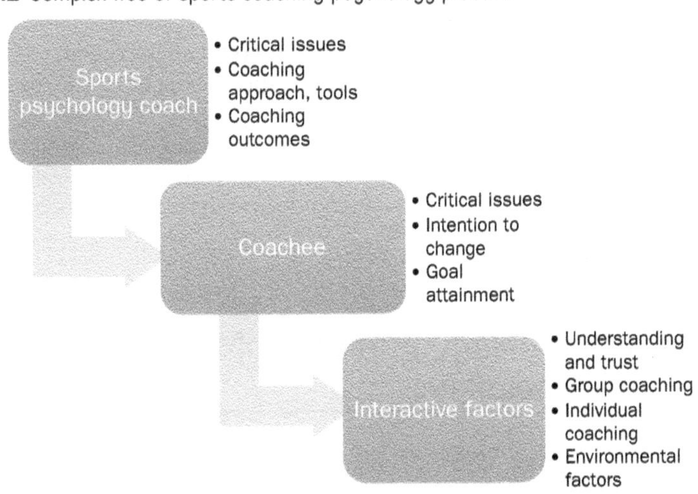

Table 7.4 Sports coaching characteristics and critical issues

Sports coaching characteristics	Critical issues: coach	Critical issues: coachee	Interactive factors
Professionally linked intervention (sports)	Knowledge and understanding – sports psychology Sports team coaching Coaching outcome delivery/goal setting Implementation and evaluation	Personal developmental needs Commitment and engagement Intention to change Goal attainment	Understanding and trust Intention and motivation to change Perceived coaching environment Organizational constraints
Managing well-being around the professional role	Sports organizational issues	Professional demands	Feedback
Performance coaching	Individual	Time, space, finance	Coaching outcomes/goal attainment

their performance in relation to sports behaviour (Berg and De Jong 2002). The coachee is the main driver to follow the relevant path using their own existing resources. Hence this can be regarded as an enabling approach (Adams 2016). The coachee's engagement with the coaching intervention process is referred to as 'pathways thinking' (Green et al. 2007). A sports coaching psychology practitioner merely provides the supportive role to enable a sports coachee's 'pathways thinking' to make a change using their own strengths and personal resources. The focus here is the application of a relevant coaching psychology practice model to plan, develop and execute sports coaching intervention for sustainable changes in performance.

An extensive discussion on sports coaching psychology is beyond the scope of this chapter, so only a few relevant key issues have been discussed here to highlight the influence of coaching psychology on developing sports coaching practice.

Coaching psychology practice informed by psychology disciplines

Different areas of psychology are not necessarily influencing the coaching psychology discipline directly, but rather the influence is subtle, at the level of theorizing and application of theory into practice. Coaching psychology is developing a rich applied groundwork using psychological constructs shared in common with other areas of psychology, for example, cognitive behavioural psychology. The discussion in this chapter has provided a few selected examples of how coaching psychology practice is informing the practical application of different areas of psychology. Coaching psychology is both informing and being informed by varied specialist psychological knowledge, thereby providing a coaching intervention platform on which practitioners can confidently deliver their practices to support individuals to reach their optimum level of functioning. The critical mass of coaching psychology is developing through this merging of knowledge across different psychology subject areas. A close look into the relationships between coaching psychology and other psychology sub-disciplines has indicated that coaching psychology is deeply embedded in the subject knowledge of different areas of psychology. More research and interdisciplinary collaboration can provide further insights into the knowledge transfer mechanisms for developing a discipline-focused application and practice in coaching psychology.

Conclusion

Coaching psychology practice is developing fast to address complex issues of developing individuals in their live environment – including in education, work, health and sports. The discussion in this chapter has drawn on relevant literature and research evidence to support arguments in favour of developing an interdisciplinary approach in coaching psychology practice. Coaching psychology will thus continue to evolve along with other areas of psychology, and it is hoped that this interdisciplinary cross-fertilization will make coaching psychology a dominant applied scientific discipline.

References

Adams, M. (2016) ENABLE: A solution-focused coaching model for individual and team coaching, *The Coaching Psychologist*, 12(1): 17–23.

Berg, I.K. and De Jong, P. (2002) *Interviewing for Solutions*. Pacific Grove, CA: Brooks/Cole.

Boysen-Rotelli, S. (2020) Executive coaching history: Growing out of organisational development, *The Coaching Psychologist*, 16(2): 26–34.

Cropley, B., Thelwell, R., Mallett, C.J. and Dieffenbach, K. (2020) Exploring sport psychology in the discipline of sports coaching, *Journal of Applied Sport Psychology*, 32(1): 1–4.

Evans, R.T. and Warren, S.G. (2019) Occupational psychology and the fire service: An introduction, in R.T. Evans and S.G. Warren (eds) *Applying Occupational Psychology to the Fire Service: Emotion, Risk and Decision Making*. Basingstoke: Palgrave Macmillan [ebook], pp. 3–10.

Figone, A. (1994) Origins of the teacher-coach role: Idealism, convenience, and unworkability, *Physical Educator*, 51(3): 148–57.

Green, L.S., Grant, A.M. and Rynsaardt, J. (2007) Evidence-based life coaching for senior high-school students: Building hardiness and hope, *International Coaching Psychology Review*, 2(1): 24–32.

Kilburg, R.R. (1996) Toward a conceptual understanding and definition of executive coaching, *Consulting Psychology Journal: Practice and Research*, 48(2): 134–44.

Kilburg, R.R. (2007) Introduction: The historical and conceptual roots of executive coaching, in R.R. Kilburg and R.C. Dietrich (eds) *The Wisdom of Coaching*. Washington, DC: American Psychological Association, pp. 3–15.

Kilburg, R.R. (2016) The development of human expertise: Toward a model for the 21st-century practice of coaching, consulting, and general applied psychology, *Consulting Psychology Journal: Practice and Research*, 68(2): 177–87.

Lee, J.A., Heberlein, E., Pyle, E. et al. (2021) Evaluation of a resiliency focused health coaching intervention for middle school students: Building resilience for healthy kids program, *American Journal of Health Promotion*, 35(3): 344–51.

Lewis, G. (1969) Adoption of the sports program, 1906–1939: The role of accommodation in the transformation of physical education, *Quest*, 12(1): 34–46.

Locke, L.F. and Massengale, J.D. (1978) Role conflict in teacher-coaches, *Research Quarterly for Exercise and Sport*, 49(2): 162–74.

Lofthouse, R., Leat, D. and Towler, C. (2010) *Coaching for Teaching and Learning: A Practical Guide for Schools*. Reading: CfBT Education Trust.

Macleod, Z.M. (2018) Thriving in higher education: Coaching women leaders, *Dissertation Abstracts International Section A: Humanities and Social Sciences*, 79(10-A) (E).

Matthewman, L.J., Nowlan, J. and Hyvönen, K. (2018) Reciprocal peer coaching: A constructivist methodology for enhancing formative assessment strategy in tertiary education, *International Coaching Psychology Review*, 13(1): 35–47.

McCarthy, P. and Giges, B. (2017) Helping coaches meet their psychological needs, in R. Thelwell, C. Harwood. and I. Greenlees (eds) *The Psychology of Sports Coaching: Research and Practice*. London: Routledge, pp. 101–13.

Millward, L. (2005) Introduction and overview: Occupational psychology paradigms, perspectives and practice, in L. Millward (ed.) *Understanding Occupational and Organisational Psychology*. London: SAGE, pp. 1–20.

Moore, M. (2021) The psychology of health in coaching. Special group in coaching psychology workshop event (online), British Psychological Society.

NHS (2021) Coaching and mentoring for leaders, NHS Leadership Academy website. Available at: https://people.nhs.uk/support-for-leaders/coaching-and-mentoring-for-leaders/ (accessed 7 September 2021).

Robinson, P.E. (2010) *Foundations of Sports Coaching*. London: Routledge.

Sage, G.H. (1987) The social world of high school athletic coaches: Multiple role demands and their consequences, *Sociology of Sport Journal*, 4(3): 213–28.

Sforzo, G.A., Kaye, M.P. and Harenberg, S. (2019) Compendium of health and wellness coaching, *American Journal of Lifestyle Medicine*, 14(2): 155–68.

Shams, M. (2015) Why is it important to understand the neurological basis of coaching intervention?, *The Coaching Psychologist*, 11(1): 28–9.

Shams, M. (2022) *Supporting the Family Business: A Coaching Practitioner's Handbook*, 2nd edn. New York: Routledge.

Sperry, L. (2013) Executive coaching and leadership assessment: Past, present, and future, *Consulting Psychology Journal: Practice and Research*, 65(4): 284–8.

Spinelli, E. and Horner, C. (2018) An existential approach to coaching psychology, in S. Palmer and A. Whybrow (eds) *Handbook of Coaching Psychology: A Guide for Practitioners*. New York: Routledge, pp. 169–79.

Spoth, J., Toman, S., Leichtman, R. and Allan, J. (2013). Gestalt approach, in J. Passmore, D.B. Peterson and T. Freire (eds) *The Wiley-Blackwell Handbook of the Psychology of Coaching and Mentoring*. Oxford: Wiley-Blackwell, pp. 385–406.

Theeboom, T., Beersma, B. and van Vianen, A.E.M. (2014) Does coaching work? A meta-analysis on the effects of coaching on individual level outcomes in an organizational context, *The Journal of Positive Psychology*, *9*(1): 1–18.

Thompson, A.D. (1987) A formative evaluation of an individualized coaching program for business managers and professionals (Doctoral dissertation, University of Minnesota), *Dissertation Abstracts International Section A: Humanities and Social Sciences*, 47: 4339.

Vadell, K. (2017) The influence of academic coaching on the retention of distance education students, *Dissertation Abstracts International Section A: Humanities and Social Sciences*, 77(10-A) (E).

van Nieuwerburgh, C. and Knight, J. (2019) Coaching in education, in S. English, J.M. Sabatine and P. Brownell (eds) *Professional Coaching: Principles and Practice*. New York: Springer, pp. 411–26.

Wood, C.L., Goodnight, C.I., Bethune, K.S., Preston, A.I. and Cleaver, S.L. (2016) Role of professional development and multi-level coaching in promoting evidence-based practice in education, *Learning Disabilities: A Contemporary Journal*, 14(2): 159–70.

The coaching client

David Tee

Summary

Much of the coaching research and practitioner literature to date has concentrated on either coaching techniques and approaches or on the relationship between the coach and the client. Very little focus has fallen upon the impact that the client as an individual has on the effectiveness of the coaching intervention. Seeking to address this gap, and drawing on evidence from counselling and therapy research, this chapter considers whether the client may actually be the single biggest determinant of coaching outcomes, which aspects of a client's personality are evidenced to have the biggest influence, and which tools may be available for coaches to apply to identify and use client factors to enhance the benefit their coaching may create.

Keywords: coaching client; common factors; client factors; active ingredients.

Introduction

One of the aspirations for the field of coaching psychology is to generate evidence that will inform how we as coaches practise our craft. In time, hopefully this evidence will extend to all aspects of our work, from ethical and reflective practice to generating and sustaining psychological safety within sessions and working with awareness of the client's organizational and wider system. One of the areas where greater understanding and evidence have been argued to be pressing for at least the last fifteen years is that of the coaching client. Bluckert (2006) raised a consideration that many practising coaches will recognize from experience: that if we treat coaching as a cure-all or silver bullet, without any consideration as to whether the proposed client is right for coaching – maybe in general, maybe with this particular coach or maybe at this particular time – there is then a risk that coaching resources will be misaligned, that suboptimal benefits will be realized and that the client in question, especially if this is their first experience of working with a coach, may talk down the value of coaching with their peers and with their direct and distal reports, resulting in a much lower take-up within that team, function area or directorate. In other words, the potentially negative consequences may extend far beyond that individual client.

In a nutshell, what this chapter is advocating is that there are (at least) two active agents in a coaching relationship. Unless we are regarding coaching as a directive intervention akin to one-to-one training or guidance, then we should assume that both client and coach are co-active in generating the focus, momentum and benefits. As we shall see, this is a conclusion that has been realized in related activities such as therapy for some time but remains little understood and researched within coaching. The hope in writing this chapter is that coaches will increasingly consider client factors in their planning and practice of coaching, all the way from chemistry meetings and matching with potential new clients through to the work in the actual coaching sessions. Pointers will be provided as to what these considerations may include, what the research evidence that does exist suggests may be sensible to bear in mind, and some tools that may be of use in working with client factors.

Before we start, let me address one objection that I have heard from some coaches. It isn't the contention that potential clients who may not be especially coachable should be written off or not invested in by their organization. Everyone should have the opportunity available to them to grow, develop and flourish in their work; we know this to be a core motivator and no one wins when such opportunities are withheld from staff. Instead, let us recognize that coaching is but one of a myriad of different developmental interventions and activities, and that different individuals may be suited to and develop more from reading a book, shadowing a colleague, progressing through a self-paced interactive learning app on their smartphone, going through a battery of assessments in a development centre or maybe enrolling for a formal qualification. Coaching simply is not the optimal solution for every person with every presenting topic in every context, however passionately we as coaches may believe in its power and effectiveness.

Case study

After a chequered CV of jobs with numerous employers, Gavin joined Acme Inc. 30 years ago in an entry-level position. He feels he knows this company very well and has enjoyed a series of promotions, finally settling at 'Head of' level, a role he has occupied for 11 years now. As Gavin is due to retire in four years' time, he has no desire to formally advance any further, but instead to see out his working days in his current job. The projected pension package more than meets his lifestyle aspirations.

Gavin looks back with pride at the many successes he has enjoyed in the past. His management style and decision-making abilities must have, he feels, played a huge role on each of these occasions. As a result of this assessment, Gavin is very confident in his own judgement. After all, why else would he have been promoted and kept in this role for so long? The only complaints he ever gets – this has happened a few times – is that he is prone to getting easily stressed when the pressure at work mounts. His staff say he can sometimes take this out on them, but he thinks they are just being too sensitive.

Gavin would argue that, in fact, his only real frustration is the lack of any performance management culture at Acme. He and his peers often joke about Human Resources being 'toothless': no one has been given a written warning for ages, let alone been fired. HR instead always seems very wary of supporting management when they raise staff performance concerns, stating that it is too difficult to address as the unions would put up a fight. Everything else, as far as Gavin is concerned, is ticking along nicely.

Outside of work, Gavin is a keen vegetable gardener and loves to spend time tending to his allotment, where he can forget about the pressures of his job, roll his sleeves up and get his hands dirty doing something practical. He considers himself an expert on ideal soil conditions for growing prize marrows and has given talks on this to allotment associations in the region. In fact, Gavin has embraced technology and even recorded a series of 'How to' gardening videos which he has uploaded to an online platform.

Time at the allotment also serves as an escape from Gavin's turbulent domestic life. His elderly parent has recently moved in and requires round-the-clock care, which is putting quite a strain on his family, all of whom are having to chip in to help. This has led to many heated arguments, which Gavin does not need right now, as he is not someone that likes to think or talk about these sorts of things. As a consequence, Gavin has started spending more and more time at the allotment, staying on to chat with his best friend of many years, Keith, rather than return home to more aggravation.

Gavin has had many bosses over the years. They never tend to last very long. The latest one, Claudette, is trying to push all her direct reports to take up coaching. Gavin doesn't really know what this is, but his mate Keith tells him that they tried it where he works and it was a waste of time. Claudette, however, raves about how much she gained from working with a coach at her last job and is really keen that her team have the same chance to benefit from coaching that she has had. Always one for a quiet life, Gavin has agreed to go along with this, so has now been assigned a coach. After all, he can go through the motions and it will all die out in a month or two when the next exciting initiative from management inevitably comes along.

- What might be some of the client factor considerations in this case study?
- If presented with this scenario, how might you determine to proceed as a coach – and why?

Client factors as an 'active coaching ingredient'

So, what is the rationale for suggesting that coaches should assume that clients vary in personality and that this might in some instances influence the coaching? I am going to make an assumption here that we are considering coaching as a human interaction: a coach–client working alliance. I am aware that coaching is increasingly becoming an activity that an individual engages in, rather than necessarily being a relationship with a human coach. Evidence of this includes self-coaching resources (Grant and Greene 2001) or AI (artificial intelligence) agents replacing human coaches (David et al. 2018), a trend that is predicted to rise through the 2020s and beyond as technology becomes more sophisticated and affordable. The client factors that influence any variance in benefit from engaging with these non-human modes of coaching may be different from the client factors we are going to be looking at in this chapter.

The early years of coaching psychology as a field of research were dominated by attempts to evidence whether or not coaching 'worked' (however that may be defined) (Briner 2012). While debates continue about the quality and reliability of the data offered up as evidence (de Haan 2021), subsequent systematic reviews and meta-analyses (such as Athanasopoulou and Dopson 2018; Wang et al. 2021) have aggregated enough data on coaching's effectiveness to at least allow the research focus to broaden to what might be the factors that make coaching work.

McKenna and Davis (2009) used the term 'active ingredients' when applying the 'common factors' therapy framework from Asay and Lambert (1999) to executive coaching. Asay and Lambert's common factors model, although not based on precise statistical analysis, is derived from a review of 60 years of research on the determinants of therapy outcomes. It suggests that 'Client variables and extratherapeutic events', which Drisko (2004) more concisely relabelled as 'the client and their context', account for 40 per cent of the variance in therapy outcome, making this the single largest categorical determinant. However, the client and their context do not account for 100 per cent of the variance, so there are three other common factors: these are labelled as 'relationship factors' (30 per cent), 'expectancy' (15 per cent) and 'techniques' (15 per cent). Although several other coaching researchers have cited this common factors model since McKenna and Davis (2009) (see Smith and Brummel 2013; MacKie 2015; O'Broin et al. 2016), this has not resulted in a large amount of research regarding what the model claims is the single largest factor: the client and their context. In fact, of the approximately 3,300 published coaching research papers detailed by Grant and O'Connor (2019), only 48 concerned the role the client plays in influencing the effectiveness of coaching, representing 1.45 per cent of the total field (Tee et al. in press). We shall return to these papers later in this chapter.

I do want to avoid reifying the McKenna and Davis common factors/active ingredients framework. Firstly, it assumes a broad equivalence between therapeutic and coaching interventions, presuming that what allows therapy to work is (at least broadly) of relevance for those wanting to understand what makes coaching effective. While these two 'helping by talking' interventions do have similarities (such as a considered setting, a ritual or procedure and the active participation of both agents), they are not identical, with their dividing line being actively researched (Giraldez-Hayes 2021). Therefore, to transpose the findings from Asay and Lambert's research on therapy across to coaching without any caveats would be bold.

Secondly, there are a number of common factors models within therapy research, dating back to Rosenzweig (1936) and including an '89 factor' model from Grencavage and Norcross (1990), so it should be recognized that the Asay and Lambert framework does not stand alone, that there are not necessarily four factors, nor that those stated in the Asay and Lambert model are definitive.

Finally, the terms used in the Asay and Lambert framework have often changed without clear explanation. For example, McKenna and Davis (2009: 246) attribute 30 per cent of the variance in outcome to 'Therapeutic Relationship Factors', a term they have taken from Asay and Lambert (1999). Yet the Asay and Lambert model is a variance on Lambert's earlier (1992) framework, which attributed 30 per cent of the outcome variance to common factors rather than to relationship factors, with the common factors being listed as therapist input skills such as warmth, empathy and acceptance. It is not made clear why these practitioner skills were subsequently recategorized as 'relationship' factors. De Haan (2021), in relating this common factors model to research on coaching, convincingly argues that we therefore probably have 76 per cent of the determinants of coaching effectiveness currently unexplained.

For all these reasons, caution is recommended in making premature claims of knowledge as to which are the factors that matter the most in making coaching work or assigning precise percentage weightings to any of them until the coaching evidence base has significantly advanced. For now, however, regardless of which version of which particular common factors model we may wish to champion, it is sufficient to point out that they all include client factors as one of the determinants. Therefore, if we are to use this chapter to consider the impact and implications of client factors on how we as coaches work, it makes sense to define what specifically we mean by the term.

Client factors have been identified by Beutler et al. (2006) as those qualities that (1) exist within the person of the client, and (2) are identifiable outside of what takes place within the intervention itself. They are 'enduring and relatively stable traits that are brought into treatment by the patient ... who is involved in the process' (Beutler et al. 2006: 13). Similarly, client factors have been defined by Cooper (2008: 62) as 'identifiable outside of what takes place in therapy (so not just the client's immediate feelings towards the therapist) and ... relatively enduring and stable ways of being'.

The terms 'enduring' and 'stable' feature in both definitions, suggesting that personality traits are a core element of the client factors construct. However, the number of client characteristics that potentially inform the process and outcome of psychotherapy is argued by Clarkin and Levy (2004) to be almost limitless. To illustrate this, they cite studies concerning personality traits (e.g. ego strength), but also objective demographic characteristics (e.g. age or gender), biological factors (e.g. REM sleep characteristics) and external characteristics (e.g. social support).

The client's wider context

Let's focus initially on those external (or 'extratherapeutic', to use the Asay and Lambert term) factors before we switch attention to the client as an individual.

Given the embryonic state of client/extratherapeutic factors research in coaching psychology, there is not a huge amount of definitive evidence as to which contextual considerations a coach should be determining when matched with a potential client. However, the notion from therapy research of a supportive environment has been transplanted to the coaching domain, with some studies focusing on the workplace culture in which the client is situated.

Redshaw's (2000) thought paper advocated supportive organizational climates as a precursor for coaching, arguing for cultures where mistakes are used as opportunities to learn and where managers typically regard coaching as a normal part of their role. Orenstein's (2002) literature review also states that the coach should consider the organization in which the client is situated and the interaction between the organization and the client, describing these considerations as a foundational premise for executive coaching.

Gormley and van Nieuwerburgh (2014) conducted a literature review on the topic of organizational culture, identifying common themes which needed to be present to support coaching. These included enrolling senior leaders as exemplar users of coaching services, publicizing success stories from clients who have benefitted from coaching, establishing a clear link between the coaching strategy and the overall organizational strategy and ensuring that coaching can be practised in a safe environment. The importance of psychological safety matters not just in the coach–client dyad, but also in a guarantee from the client's organization concerning the confidentiality of the whole process (Rekalde et al. 2015).

In principle, this means a client might be perfectly suited to coaching as their optimal developmental intervention, but the context in which they work may act as a counterforce. Coaching session attendance may repeatedly be pulled by management due to competing considerations, fresh ideas generated by the client in a coaching session may be seen as a threat to their immediate line manager's authority or status, or the wider organizational culture may be highly risk-averse and stifle any innovation or creativity. At the very least, coaches should be discussing the wider context with their client. It may be that there is sufficient information to suggest that any time and money invested in coaching may struggle to generate the intended benefit. Rather than the coach reacting by seeing any such adverse conditions as a test of their powers, there may be a case that they instead signpost the client to alternative activities more likely to generate value.

Objective and inferred client factors

Beyond the context in which the coaching is taking place, individual client factors are typically divided into two broad categories. 'Objective factors' include the individual's demographic or physical attributes, whereas most of the research focuses on 'inferred factors': qualities that cannot directly be observed and which may be psychological constructs. Such studies typically concern personality traits – particularly those that are measurable using psychometric tools.

Decades of funded research means much more is known about the role of objective client factors in the related practice of therapy than is presently understood in coaching. These have included studies regarding age, gender, ethnicity, sexual orientation and socio-economic status, among other attributes. In addition, different objective factors have been researched for different classifications of mental health disorder. Interested readers are referred to Castonguay and Beutler (2006) for details about some of the specific studies. Within coaching research, a study by Bozer et al. (2015) indicates that male executives experience a greater enhancement in self-awareness when working with male coaches. Related to this, Tamir and Finfer (2016) suggest that clients aged 40 or older demonstrated greater self-reflection than those aged 39 and below, as well as more noticeable degrees of change. Finally, several studies (including Lam 2016; Dodds and Grajfoner 2018) identified the effects that a client's cultural background may have on how they work with their coach. For example, some cultures may expect a high level of relational trust, greater power distance or a higher amount of direction than a coach may typically build into the way they work. In time, objective factors other than cultural background, gender or age might also be examined in a coaching context.

In addition to research on these objective client factors, a wide range of inferred client factors have been studied, with the sheer variety of personality traits that have been examined pointing to the absence of a shared agenda within the coaching research community. A targeted focus in the coming years on generating more robust studies on those factors where emerging data indicates they are of some significance will help advance our understanding about who is most likely to benefit from coaching. Bsharah (2018) presents typical current practice about suitability as simply an informal discussion that may be conducted by the coach, maybe the client's line manager or maybe perhaps a representative from the organization's Human Resources, which is held with the potential client on what they hope the coaching will achieve. With a focused research agenda, it should be plausible in the next few years to identify a proportion of evidence-based coaching client factors which would allow an improvement on this current practice in determining coachability. I will therefore point to those factors which already have supporting empirical evidence in the next section of this chapter.

What the research currently indicates

As mentioned, a lot of different personality traits have been researched over the last few decades, meaning that our state of knowledge right now is that there are many areas where we have some evidence of a link between the presence of that trait in an employee and the likelihood that coaching is the best intervention to aid them in making meaningful progress towards a desired outcome. What follows may raise more questions than provide answers, as most of these client factors only have one or two studies thus far associated with them and the study designs may often be open to critical challenge, but this is an accurate summation of the evidence that coaching research to date has generated.

These findings are based on a systematic review, argued to be the '"gold standard" way to synthesize the findings of several studies investigating the same question' (Dickson et al. 2014: 3). It follows a rigorous, defined process that involves collaboration across several researchers to minimize the risk of bias creeping into the results, and a thorough interrogation of everything that meets defined inclusion criteria – in this instance, scrutinizing some 23,000 pieces of published research.

A systematic review of a diagnosable medical condition, such as obesity or dementia, is straightforward. One can filter through the research databases using the relevant objectively defined term and feel confident that the search results accurately contain all relevant studies. This is not the case in coaching research. Not only do we have a situation where coaching is variously defined and practised, but numerous actual and faux synonyms have been introduced to describe the person who uses coaching. The term 'client' has been the standard term across the 'helping by talking' interventions for decades. Additionally, in coaching, it is codified in key documents, such as the Global Code of Ethics (2021), advocated by numerous national and international signatory professional coaching bodies as the term used to describe the individual who accesses coaching services. However, a search just for studies about coaching clients would omit those papers that introduce alternative terms ('executive', 'player', 'coachee', 'learner' and more) to describe the coaching client. This means any review of client factor research has to search for every study with the term 'coach' in it to ensure all these substitute terms for client are captured. One important plea for any current or future researchers reading this chapter, therefore, is to please use the standard term 'client' when disseminating your findings, so that it becomes easier for us to aggregate our knowledge and understanding.

Tee et al. (in press) screened the initial 23,000 studies to look for those in the medium of English and published in peer-reviewed journals. We included only those papers that consider coaching where the coach held no supervisory authority over the client and where one or more client factors were featured as variables in quantitative research or emerged as themes in qualitative research. We limited our findings to those that generated primary empirical data and featured clients of working age, described as neurotypically functioning and engaged in one-to-one, face-to-face coaching. This ultimately reduced the total number of eligible studies to the 48 hinted at earlier in this chapter. Within these studies, there was statistical evidence for the role of 18 coaching client factors having an impact on the effectiveness of the coaching, as detailed in Table 8.1.

Some of the client factors are recognized traits widely researched in psychology studies interested in individual differences. Self-esteem, locus of control and extraversion would be clear examples, and it may be that such factors are those most defensible to explore further as we advance our understanding in the next few years. There are other traits that may be specific to the particular research team that conducted an individual study, such as 'executive

Table 8.1 Source papers and definitions of all client factors statistically evidenced as impacting on the effectiveness of workplace coaching

Client factor	Sources of evidence	Definitions taken from the literature
Age	Blackman and Moscardo 2012; Tamir and Finfer 2016	The number of years an individual has lived.
Change readiness	MacKie 2015	An individual's ability to engage in and benefit from attempts at change.
Commitment	Boyce et al. 2010; Gan and Chong 2015; Lim et al. 2019	An individual's dedication to perform the work related to the coaching engagement that eventually will translate directly into behavioural performance.
Conscientiousness	Stewart et al. 2008	An individual's propensity for planning, organizing, carrying out tasks, and for being reliable, purposeful, strong-willed and determined.
Developmental self-efficacy	Bozer and Joo 2015; Bozer et al. 2013	An individual's personal beliefs about their capabilities to learn.
Emotional stability	Schermuly 2018; Stewart et al. 2008	An individual's tendency towards being calm, even-tempered and relaxed, and their ability to face stressful situations without upset.
Executive involvement	Smith and Brummel 2013	An individual's willingness to (1) invest time and energy in the process, (2) do the work of development even when it becomes difficult and (3) take personal responsibility for transferring what is learned into action for change on the job.
Extraversion	Jones et al. 2014	An individual's tendency towards warmth, gregariousness, assertiveness, activity, excitement-seeking and positive emotions.
Feedback receptivity	Bozer and Joo 2015; Bozer et al. 2013; McEnrue et al. 2009	An individual's predisposition to seek and use feedback.

(*continued*)

Table 8.1 *(continued)*

Client factor	Sources of evidence	Definitions taken from the literature
Gender	Bozer et al. 2015	The range of characteristics pertaining to, and differentiating between, masculinity and femininity. Depending on the context, these characteristics may include biological sex, sex-based social structures or gender identity.
Generalized self-efficacy	Cantrell and Hughes 2008; de Haan et al. 2013, 2016; Duckworth and de Haan 2009; Lim et al. 2019; McEnrue et al. 2009; Mosteo et al. 2015; Stewart et al. 2008	An individual's expectations of mastery in new situations.
Learning goal-orientation	Bozer and Joo 2015; Bozer et al. 2013; Scriffignano 2011	An individual's desire to increase their competence by developing new skills and mastering new situations.
Locus of control	MacKie 2015	An individual's confidence in being able to control outcomes.
Motivation	Bozer et al. 2013; Schermuly 2018; Sonesh et al. 2015	A set of energetic forces that originates both within as well as beyond an individual's being, to initiate behaviour and to determine its form, direction, intensity and duration.
Openness to experience	McEnrue et al. 2009; Stewart et al. 2008	An individual's curiosity about their inner and outer worlds, their willingness to entertain novel ideas and unconventional values, and the intensity with which they experience their emotions.
Self-esteem	MacKie 2015	The overall value that an individual places on themselves as a person.
Self-presentation ability	Rank and Gray 2017	An individual's tailoring of their actions in accordance with immediate situational cues.
Unconditional self-acceptance	Ellam-Dyson and Palmer 2011	The individual fully and unconditionally accepts themselves whether or not they behave intelligently, correctly or competently and whether or not other people approve, respect or love them.

involvement'. These novel terms may overlap with or be approximations of other traits or behaviours that are more widely considered and where a bank of existing evidence from fields other than coaching science may offer illumination. I would state that, a few years on from now when our understanding of client factors is greater, it is unlikely that each of these 18 factors will have been found to make an identical contribution. Therefore, we can improve our understanding and practice of coaching by using this list as a starting point: rather than adding a 19th or a 32nd new variable to our menu of client factor considerations, we might instead seek to consolidate and confirm (or otherwise) the role that these already evidenced factors might actually play. In addition, coaches – and prospective clients – can use this as a checklist for auditing where there are enabling client factors present and where there may be gaps that need to be worked around, such as an initial absence of change readiness (a willingness to let go of familiar or proven strategies that have served the client well in the past) or a low commitment to the coaching process. These could point to pre-coaching activities to ready the client for engagement with their first session, to the initial focus of work in those early coaching sessions or even to alternative development interventions more suited to that individual.

Working with client factors

To recap, we have considered how the focus in coaching research has switched from whether coaching works to which factors make it work. We have looked at the strong influence that Asay and Lambert's (1999) common factors model has had on coaching studies in the last decade and that there are a number of 'common factor models' within therapy research, but they all identify the role that the individual client and their context play on influencing the effectiveness of any intervention. Given this consensus, we have shared the 18 client factors where there is already some statistical evidence that these do have an impact on the effectiveness of workplace coaching. Considering the importance of coaching client factors, let's next examine a number of tools that already exist with the intention to help coaches and those responsible for coaching activity in organizations identify staff who have the greatest chance of benefitting from access to coaching.

We will begin with a practitioner tool. Type 'coachability index' into Google and you will find an identically worded questionnaire being publicly offered by multiple commercial coaching providers, several of whom each claim copyright on this instrument. It asks a short series of questions of any potential client, such as whether they are willing to share the credit for their success with their coach. The individual totals up their answers to give them a single score which is claimed to determine for them whether they are not coachable, coachable or very coachable. This is a simple questionnaire, with no visible evidence as to how these questions were identified to be reliable, valid predictors of coachability.

We mentioned Bluckert (2006) at the start of this chapter, restating his warning about the dangers of imposing coaching on all staff across a layer of management or within a work team, regardless of individual differences in suitability. Recognizing that there was (and probably still is in 2022) a pressing need to increase our understanding of the client factors that do make a difference, Bluckert offered a framework (see Table 8.2) featuring six factors argued to impact on coachability. Bluckert made no claim that this was based on any systematic research, but did nonetheless consider them critical success factors.

Given Bluckert's modest claims about this tool as a diagnostic device, it seems churlish to be too critical about it as anything other than what he intended it to be: a catalyst for further understanding about client factors. Nonetheless, as a practical tool that a coach might wish to adopt, it does raise several questions. For instance, relatively uncontroversially, Bluckert emboldens the left-hand column to emphasize the presence or absence of severe psychological problems as the prime consideration. However, is this to mean that each of the remaining coachability factors are all equally weighted? Is, for instance, a high level of interpersonal problems automatically of equal consequence to a person's coachability as a high threat of career derailment? Might it be instead mediated by, for example, the job role the prospective coaching client holds and that role's requirement for good interpersonal relationships? And, while a client whose diagnosis might fit them neatly along one row in Bluckert's table can be assigned a clear coachability level, what of those clients – probably the majority of people – whose profile might zigzag from column to column? Those who may have absent career derailment threats, medium motivation for coaching and poor perception of others? What conclusion is the coach to reach about that individual's coachability?

Bluckert's coachability table therefore serves us best as a catalyst for client suitability consideration: a set of prompts for reflection rather than a formal diagnostic tool. In a similar vein, Wasylyshyn (2020) proposes a series of a dozen factors that she suggests may indicate whether it is appropriate to instigate coaching with a particular client. Wasyslyshyn's framework (see Table 8.3) relates closely to the evidenced client factors of motivation and commitment (Table 8.1). She highlights a category of client, the 'faker', who seems willing to engage with coaching but who has no intention of actually making any change. This may be because the coaching has been initiated by someone in the organization with significant authority, so the individual feels a compulsion to 'go along with it'. It may possibly be related to excessive narcissism, characterized by Wasylyshyn (2020: 36) as 'a tendency to define reality to suit themselves, masking their weaknesses with defensive reasoning and projecting blame onto others, limited interpersonal skills and rigid thinking based on former patterns of problem-solving'.

Regardless of the motivations of that individual, Wasylyshyn's argument is that they can be identified and that company resource on coaching can be far better redirected towards other staff where the likelihood of a return on that investment is much greater. Considering the criteria in Table 8.3, there are a number of factors that the coach should be able to make an informed judgement about in the first one or two sessions. These include the client's ability to be vulnerable or to introspect, as well as the extent to which they are prioritizing

Table 8.2 Coachability levels

Severe psychological problems	Interpersonal problems	Perception of others	Threat of career derailment	Performance issues	Motivation for coaching	Coachability level
Absent	Absent/low	Excellent/ good	Absent	Absent	High	Excellent
Absent	Absent/low	Excellent/ good	Absent/low	Absent/low	Medium/high	Good
Absent	Low/medium	Medium	Low/medium	Low/medium	Medium	Average
Absent	Medium/high	Medium/ poor	Medium/high	Medium/high	Variable: low–high	Poor
High	High	Poor	High	High	Variable: low–high	Inappropriate to intervene right now

Adapted from Bluckert (2006: 34)

Table 8.3 Comparison of ideal executive coaching participants versus 'fakers'

Factors	Ideal executive coaching participants	'Fakers'
Initiation of executive coaching	By the client (if not by the client, he/she is receptive and enthusiastic when coaching is suggested)	By the company
Intention to participate	High	Limited to low
Narcissism	Appropriate, productive	Excessive, unproductive
Emotional intelligence	Medium-high	Low
Career aspiration	High; recognize need to keep evolving as leaders	High; consider selves fully evolved as leaders
Positional power	High; does not foster resistance to coaching	High; fosters defensive resistance to coaching
Prioritization of coaching	High	Low
Chemistry with coach	High; form strong working alliance	Low: hard for coach to break through resistance
Compliance in coaching	Real; client has strong development intention	Feigned for 'political' reasons
Capacity for introspection	Moderate–high	Low
Ability to be vulnerable	Moderate–high	Low
Openness about having a coach	High	Low

Adapted from Wasylyshyn (2020: 40)

and making progress on the focus of the coaching both within and between sessions.

Let's look at one final framework, this time based on data from a qualitative research study by Kretzschmar (2010). Labelled the 'Coaching Client Readiness Model', Kretzschmar's framework details six topics for diagnosis or consideration based on both individual and contextual client factors (see Figure 8.1). These were determined from interviews with actual and potential clients, as well as coaches. The data interrogation resulted in the following six themes, which Kretzschmar proposes as having positive or negative ripple effects on one another: the effect of the first theme may be such that the following five themes do not even become considerations for some potential clients.

The readiness model begins with issues of culture and class. It may be that the situation has changed since 2010, when coaching was often seen as the preserve of the C-suite. While there are countries and sectors where this

Figure 8.1 Coaching Client Readiness Model

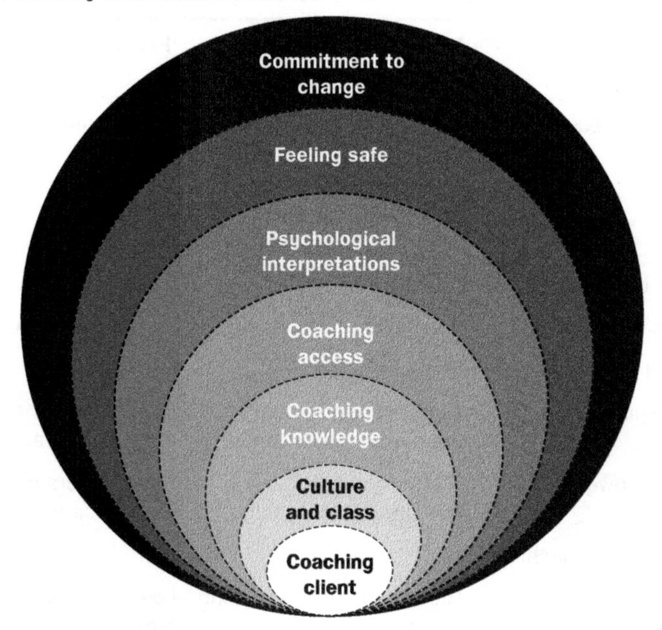

Adapted from Kretzschmar (2010: 7)

assumption may still be the case, the increase in digital coaching and its positive effect on affordability have democratized access to coaching across far more layers in the workplace in many organizations in the last decade. Nonetheless, coaching as a one-to-one, client-led, developmental intervention may still be perceived as predominantly accessed by white-collar, service sector professionals. There is still an opportunity for more workplaces, education settings and communities to be given the means to harness the benefits and impact that coaching can generate.

The second theme is knowledge about coaching. As this is an unlicensed industry where service providers variously define and practise what they badge as 'coaching', sometimes even using their technical knowledge or years served in industry as part of their differentiated offering in what is supposed to be a non-directive intervention, it is understandable why some buyers might be confused as to what coaching is. In addition, Kretzschmar found that coaches, immersed in the subject, often overestimated the number of people who had even heard of coaching. There must have been a shift in awareness levels in the intervening years since 2010, but not such a shift that we should assume this issue no longer exists anywhere.

Access to coaching involved having sufficient budget and time: for busy executives, the latter may be the main perceived barrier, whereas for tactical and operative staff it may be the former. This can be exacerbated by a company's coaching policy. If coaching is used, for instance, to drive a talent retention strategy, then certain potential clients may be prioritized over others, even if the latter are more coachable and therefore more likely to benefit.

Two of the three remaining readiness themes relate to inferred client factors that have recurred several times in this chapter: readiness and commitment to change. Kretzschmar says a client's readiness is largely determined by their psychological interpretation of themselves, which may be informed by their willingness to be completely open and honest (Wasylyshyn's notion of 'vulnerability'). If this is coupled with a healthy self-esteem, a positive attitude, a willingness to reflect on feedback and a level of emotional stability, then blockages such as fear and anxiety are less likely to emerge and inhibit engagement in coaching.

Commitment to change is enhanced by a compelling reason, be this a need for greater values alignment, an inability to tolerate the status quo and its consequences or a motivating ideal future that acts to energize the client's resources and efforts. Kretzschmar also highlights the importance of the client being able to take responsibility, also echoed in Wasyslyshyn's framework as crucially low or absent among 'faker' clients.

The other factor, 'feeling safe', may be in part but not wholly determined by the individual client. The coach would also need input skills such as the ability to build rapport or reassure the client about the levels of psychological safety they will experience. Additionally, the wider context in which the client is situated is crucial here. Do their family and friends support them in their desire to engage with coaching? What about their peers and immediate line manager at work? What is the prevailing culture around learning and development in their organization? Is coaching stigmatized or viewed as remedial by any of these stakeholders within the client's system? A hostile or negative attitude by one of these individuals or groupings may be sufficient to undermine all the remaining 'readiness' factors in the client's favour. Interested readers are encouraged to source Kretzschmar's article, where she provides 45 prompt questions relating to these six client readiness themes, intended as an aid for the coach's own diagnostic reflective thinking rather than for a client to complete and score themselves.

Conclusion

Decades of research within related helping-by-talking professions point to the important role that individual differences, or 'client factors', play in influencing the likelihood of benefits being realized from any given coaching engagement. An assumption that clients do not play a role in the effectiveness of coaching – that it is all about the coach and a test of their powers – takes us back to Bluckert's (2006) warning about the ethical and pragmatic consequences such a mindset may generate.

While the research evidence promisingly points to a range of interesting and plausible client traits that seem to be having some influence on coachability, there is – as yet – no formal diagnostic tool available for coaches and organizational sponsors to use with prospective clients. However, we have explored a range of frameworks informed by practice and research data and where there are some emerging areas of consensus, such as the central role that client commitment to the process and willingness to change existing behaviours and strategies may play. These frameworks, either adopted wholesale, blended or used as a catalyst by coaches to shape their own bespoke checklists of consideration based on their typical approaches and client bases, may serve as useful inputs for reflective practice. They also speak to the more formal practice of formulation, long advocated by Corrie and Kovacs (2022) and others as a hallmark of expert practice. Here, the coach can draw on how the client presents and the subjective narrative and behaviour they offer, alongside other inputs including the practitioner's bank of experience and analysis, to generate an informed and explanatory account which may point to recommendations as to whether it is ethical to proceed with coaching with this particular individual.

Ultimately, if we believe that the client is an active agent in the coaching process and that not all clients are identical, then should it matter that, for this particular person at this particular time, coaching may not be the optimal intervention for them? If we are passionate advocates for lifelong growth, learning and development, and it so happens that this potential client will gain more by being signposted to an activity other than coaching, as long as they and their organization realize the impact and benefits from that alternative intervention, then we as coaches can be more effectively redeployed where we are most likely to generate a desired and lasting beneficial change.

Prompts for possible reflection

- What is your current practice in determining coaching as the optimum intervention for potential clients?
- What are some of the objective or inferred qualities in clients you have worked with to date that have impacted on their engagement with and benefit from coaching?
- Similarly, what have been the contextual or 'extratherapeutic' factors that have enabled or inhibited individual clients?
- In your experience as a practitioner, is coachability more about the presence of positive client factors or the absence of negative client factors?
- What are the implications of these reflections and the evidence in this chapter on how you might evolve your future coaching practice?

References

Asay, T.P. and Lambert, M.J. (1999) The empirical case for the common factors in therapy: Quantitative findings, in M.A. Hubble, B.L. Duncan and S.D. Miller (eds) *The Heart and Soul of Change: What Works in Therapy*. Washington, DC: American Psychological Association, pp. 23–55.

Athanasopoulou, A. and Dopson, S. (2018) A systematic review of executive coaching outcomes: Is it the journey or the destination that matters the most?, *The Leadership Quarterly*, 29(1): 70–88. https://doi.org/10.1016/j.leaqua.2017.11.004

Beutler, L.E., Blatt, S.J., Alimohamed, S., Levy, K.N. and Angtuaco, L. (2006) Participant factors in treating dysphoric disorders, in L.G. Castonguay and L.E. Beutler (eds) *Principles of Therapeutic Change that Work.* New York: Oxford University Press, pp. 13–63.

Blackman, A. and Moscardo, G. (2012) Exploring the coaching experience: Analysing coachee perspectives on factors contributing to coaching effectiveness, in P. Lindvall and D. Megginson (eds) *Developing Mentoring and Coaching Research and Practice.* Sheffield: European Mentoring and Coaching Council, pp. 5–19.

Bluckert, P. (2006) *Psychological Dimensions of Executive Coaching.* Maidenhead: Open University Press.

Boyce, L.A., Jeffrey Jackson, R. and Neal, L.J. (2010) Building successful leadership coaching relationships: Examining impact of matching criteria in a leadership coaching program, *Journal of Management Development*, 29(10): 914–31. https://doi.org/10.1108/02621711011084231

Bozer, G. and Joo, B.K. (2015) The effects of coachee characteristics and coaching relationships on feedback receptivity and self-awareness in executive coaching, *International Leadership Journal*, 7(3): 36–58.

Bozer, G., Joo, B.K. and Santora, J.C. (2015) Executive coaching – does coach–coachee matching based on similarity really matter?, *Consulting Psychology Journal: Practice and Research*, 67(3): 218–33. https://doi.org/10.1037/cpb0000044

Bozer, G., Sarros, J.C. and Santora, J. C. (2013) The role of coachee characteristics in executive coaching for effective sustainability, *Journal of Management Development*, 32(3): 277–94. https://doi.org/10.1108/02621711311318319

Briner, R.B. (2012) Does coaching work and does anyone really care?, *OP Matters*, 16: 4–11. Available at: http://www.cebma.org/wp-content/uploads/Briner-Does-Coaching-Work-OP-Matters-2012.pdf (accessed 16 May 2022).

Bsharah, J. (2018) Understanding developmental readiness for the process of executive coaching: Stakeholders' views. Unpublished doctoral dissertation, Fielding Graduate University, Santa Barbara, CA.

Cantrell, S.C. and Hughes, H.K. (2008) Teacher efficacy and content literacy implementation: An exploration of the effects of extended professional development with coaching, *Journal of Literacy Research*, 40(1): 95–127. https://doi.org/10.1080/10862960802070442

Castonguay, L.G. and Beutler, L.E. (eds) (2006) *Principles of Therapeutic Change that Work.* New York: Oxford University Press.

Clarkin, J.F. and Levy, K.N. (2004) The influence of client variables on psychotherapy, in M.J. Lambert (ed.) *Bergin and Garfield's Handbook of Psychotherapy and Behavior Change*, 5th edn. New York: John Wiley & Sons, pp. 194–226.

Cooper, M. (2008) *Essential Research Findings in Counselling and Psychotherapy.* London: Sage Publications.

Corrie, S. and Kovacs, L. (2022) Addressing the self-care needs of coaches through the use of formulation, *Coaching: An International Journal of Theory, Research and Practice*, 15(1): 117–30. doi: 10.1080/17521882.2021.1926523

David, O.A., Şoflău, R. and Matu, S. (2018) Technology and coaching, in M.E. Bernard and O.A. David (eds) *Coaching for Rational Living: Theory, Techniques and Applications*. Cham: Springer, pp. 199–209.

de Haan, E. (2021) *What Works in Executive Coaching.* Abingdon: Routledge.

de Haan, E., Duckworth, A., Birch, D. and Jones, C. (2013) Executive coaching outcome research: The contribution of common factors such as relationship, personality match, and self-efficacy, *Consulting Psychology Journal: Practice and Research*, 65(1): 40–57. http://dx.doi.org/10.1037/a0031635

de Haan, E., Grant, A.M., Burger, Y. and Eriksson, P.O. (2016) A large-scale study of executive and workplace coaching: The relative contributions of relationship, personality match, and self-efficacy, *Consulting Psychology Journal: Practice and Research*, 68(3): 189–207. http://dx.doi.org/10.1037/cpb0000058

Dickson, R., Cherry, M.G. and Boland, A. (2014) Carrying out a systematic review as a master's thesis, in A. Boland, M.G. Cherry and R. Dickson (eds) *Doing a Systematic Review*. London: Sage, pp. 1–16.

Dodds, G. and Grajfoner, D. (2018) Executive coaching and national culture in the United Arab Emirates: An interpretative phenomenological analysis, *International Coaching Psychology Review*, 13(1): 89–105.

Drisko, J.W. (2004) Common factors in psychotherapy outcome: Meta-analytic findings and their implications for practice and research, *Families in Society*, 85(1): 81–90. https://doi.org/10.1606/1044-3894.239

Duckworth, A. and de Haan, E. (2009) What clients say about our coaching, *Training Journal*, August: 64–7.

Ellam-Dyson, V. and Palmer, S. (2011) Leadership coaching? No thanks, I'm not worthy, *The Coaching Psychologist*, 7(2): 108–17.

Gan, G.C. and Chong, C.W. (2015) Coaching relationship in executive coaching: A Malaysian study, *Journal of Management Development*, 34(4): 476–93. https://doi.org/10.1108/JMD-08-2013-0104

Giraldez Hayes, A. (2021) Different domains or grey areas? Setting boundaries between coaching and therapy: A thematic analysis, *The Coaching Psychologist*, 17(2): 18–29.

Global Code of Ethics (2021) *Global Code of Ethics for Coaches, Mentors, and Supervisors*. Available at: https://emccuk.org/Common/Uploaded%20files/Policies/Global_Code_of_Ethics_EN_v3.pdf (accessed 16 May 2022).

Gormley, H. and van Nieuwerburgh, C. (2014) Developing coaching cultures: A review of the literature, *Coaching: An International Journal of Theory, Research and Practice*, 7(2): 90–101. https://doi.org/10.1080/17521882.2014.915863

Grant, A.M. and Greene, J. (2001) *Coach Yourself: Make Real Change in Your Life*. Harlow: Pearson Education.

Grant, A.M. and O'Connor, S. (2019) A brief primer for those new to coaching research and evidence-based practice, *The Coaching Psychologist*, 15(1): 3–10.

Grencavage, L.M. and Norcross, J.C. (1990) Where are the commonalities among the therapeutic common factors?, *Professional Psychology: Research and Practice*, 21(5): 372–8. http://dx.doi.org/10.1037/0735-7028.21.5.372

Jones, R., Woods, S. and Hutchinson, E. (2014) The influence of the Five Factor Model of personality on the perceived effectiveness of executive coaching, *International Journal of Evidence Based Coaching and Mentoring*, 12(2): 109–18. Available at: https://radar.brookes.ac.uk/radar/items/122ac5f8-7445-4280-8aa4-e3a14a38dce2/1 (accessed 16 May 2022).

Kretzschmar, I. (2010) Exploring clients' readiness for coaching, *International Journal of Evidence Based Coaching and Mentoring*, Special Issue 4: 1–20. https://doi.org/10.24384/IJEBCM/S4

Lam, P. (2016) Chinese culture and coaching in Hong Kong, *International Journal of Evidence Based Coaching and Mentoring*, 14(1): 57–73. https://doi.org/ 10.24384/IJEBCM/14/1

Lambert, M.J. (1992) Implications of outcome research for psychotherapy integration, in J.C. Norcross and M.R. Goldstein (eds) *Handbook of Psychotherapy Integration*. New York: Basic Books, pp. 94–129.

Lim, D.H., Oh, E., Ju, B. and Kim, H.N. (2019) Mediating role of career coaching on job-search behavior of older generations, *The International Journal of Aging and Human Development*, 88(1): 82–104. https://doi.org/10.1177/0091415017743009

MacKie, D. (2015) The effects of coachee readiness and core self-evaluations on leadership coaching outcomes: A controlled trial, *Coaching: An International Journal of Theory, Research and Practice*, 8(2): 120–36. https://doi.org/10.1080/17521882.2015.1019532

McEnrue, M.P., Groves, K.S. and Shen, W. (2009) Emotional intelligence development – leveraging individual characteristics, *Journal of Management Development*, 28(2): 150–74. https://doi.org/10.1108/02621710910932106

McKenna, D.D. and Davis, S.L. (2009) Hidden in plain sight: The active ingredients of executive coaching, *Industrial and Organizational Psychology*, 2(3): 244–60. https://doi.org/10.1111/j.1754-9434.2009.01143.x

Mosteo, L.P., Batista-Foguet, J.M., Mckeever, J.D. and Serlavós, R. (2015) Understanding cognitive-emotional processing through a coaching process, *The Journal of Applied Behavioral Science*, 52(1): 64–96. https://doi.org/10.1177/0021886315600070

O'Broin, A., Spaten, O.M. and Løkken, L.O. (2016) The quest for research in the coaching relationship, *Coaching Psykologi – The Danish Journal of Coaching Psychology*, 5(1): 75–82. https://doi.org/10.5278/ojs.cp.v5i1.1687

Orenstein, R.L. (2002) Executive coaching: It's not just about the executive, *The Journal of Applied Behavioural Sciences*, 38(3): 355–74. https://doi.org/10/1177/0021886302038003006.

Rank, J. and Gray, D. (2017) The role of coaching for relationship satisfaction, self-reflection, and self-esteem, *Consulting Psychology Journal: Practice and Research*, 69(3): 187–208. https://doi.org/10.1037/cpb0000082

Redshaw, B. (2000) Do we really understand coaching? How can we make it work better?, *Industrial & Commercial Training*, 32(3): 106–8. https://doi.org/10.1108/00197850010371693.

Rekalde, I., Landeta, J. and Albizu, E. (2015) Determining factors in the effectiveness of executive coaching as a management development tool, *Management Decision*, 53(8): 1677–97. https://doi.org/10.1108/MD-12-2014-0666.

Rosenzweig, S. (1936) Some implicit common factors in diverse methods of psychotherapy, *American Journal of Orthopsychiatry*, 6(3): 412–15. https://doi.org/10.1111/j.1939-0025.1936.tb05248.x

Schermuly, C.C. (2018) Client dropout from business coaching, *Consulting Psychology Journal: Practice and Research*, 70(3): 250–67. https://doi.org/10.1037/cpb0000112

Scriffignano, R.S. (2011) Coaching within organisations: Examining the influence of goal orientation on leaders' professional development, *Coaching: An International Journal of Theory, Research and Practice*, 4(1): 20–31. https://doi.org/10.1080/17521882.2010.550898

Smith, I.M. and Brummel, B.J. (2013) Investigating the role of the active ingredients in executive coaching, *Coaching: An International Journal of Theory, Research and Practice*, 6(1): 57–71. https://doi.org/10.1080/17521882.2012.758649

Sonesh, S.C., Coultas, C.W., Lacerenza, C.N., Marlow, S.L., Benishek, L.E. and Salas, E. (2015). The power of coaching: A meta-analytic investigation, *Coaching: An International Journal of Theory, Research and Practice*, 8(2): 73–95. https://doi.org/10.1080/17521882.2015.1071 418

Stewart, L.J., Palmer, S., Wilkin, H. and Kerrin, M. (2008) The influence of character: Does personality impact coaching success?, *International Journal of Evidence Based Coaching and Mentoring*, 6(1): 32–42. https://doi.org/10.24384/IJEBCM/6/1

Tamir, L.M. and Finfer, L.A. (2016) Executive coaching: The age factor, *Consulting Psychology Journal: Practice and Research*, 68(4): 313–25. https://doi.org/10.1037/cpb0000069

Tee, D., Misra, K., Roderique-Davis, G. and Shearer, D. (in press) A systematic review of coaching client characteristics, *International Coaching Psychology Review*, 17(1).

Wang, Q., Lai, Y.L., Xu, X. and McDowall, A. (2021) The effectiveness of workplace coaching: A meta-analysis of contemporary psychologically informed coaching approaches, *Journal of Work-Applied Management*. https://doi.org/10.1108/JWAM-04-2021-0030
Wasylyshyn, K.M. (2020) A road resisted: 'Fakers' in executive coaching and how to avoid wasting company resources on them, *The Coaching Psychologist*, 16(1): 34–40.

Further reading

Bohart, A.C. and Tallman, K. (1999) *How Clients Make Therapy Work*. Washington, DC: American Psychological Association.
Haden, S. (2013) *It's Not About the Coach*. Winchester: John Hunt Publishing.

Coaching psychology practice in a changing society

Manfusa Shams

Summary

The most recent changes in work practice are 'hybrid work', 'virtual work' and working from home using advanced technologies (online). Using relevant research evidence, this chapter offers critical discussion on the delivery of coaching practice for individuals engaged in 'hybrid work', remote work and virtual work. The discussion also extends to include the important issue of localized and global coaching.

The chapter presents the application of coaching psychology to the changing needs of individuals. These include the new way of working resulting from the Covid-19 pandemic and with other environmental hazards in a local and global context. The increasing applications of coaching psychology practice to major areas of society, along with the need to recognize coaching psychology practice as an implementation science, are also highlighted.

Keywords: hybrid work, virtual coaching, coaching psychology, global coaching, local context, coaching psychology practice, implementation science.

Introduction

The predominance of modern technology, affordable and available virtual platforms and tools is leading to an alternative professional coaching practice in which advanced technologies and artificial intelligence are likely to accelerate coaching practice, but not to the exclusion of a human presence as a coaching practitioner. This chapter presents critical discussion in this area using existing evidence-based research and recent developments. The new concept of 'hybrid work' offers a changing landscape for coaching practitioners, especially in the light of challenging issues around the conventional work model in which visible human presence is considered mandatory to highly efficient performance and high-quality production. The chapter focuses on the major critical issues relating to the recent changes in life and working styles, particularly the technology-aided working environment with less 'in person presence'. The discussion is supported by selected examples of coaching psychology contributions to society, taking into consideration of diversity in coaching practice across the world.

Aims

The aim of this chapter is to inform readers about the promising and changing nature of coaching practice, and the need to align coaching practice with the challenging environmental demands to support individuals' development.

Hybrid work and coaching practice

'Hybrid work' refers to a type of flexible working conditions, using both remote and conventional office work, where autonomy and personal choices are offered to an individual to work at their own pace. A 'hybrid work' model was imposed widely in the two years from 2020 as a result of the Covid-19 pandemic all over the world. The forced implementation of a hybrid work style has gradually taken over the conventional working structure. This change in work behaviour has shown individuals' capabilities for adaptation and adjustment in relation to the changing environment. While hybrid work may be economically beneficial for employers, it also has a downside effect because of the resulting impersonal nature of interaction with others in the workplace, and psychosocial risk factors (isolation, lack of reinforcement, motivation, absence of live teamwork) affecting performance and well-being.

In the context of non-conventional/remote work, a coaching practitioner has a major task to deliver coaching using relevant psychological models for which human functioning at the optimum level will be the prime focus of the coaching intervention. There is no evidence-based literature about the most effective approach in coaching intervention for hybrid work as it is still a new working model under consideration for employees and employers, and it may even be a temporary replacement for conventional office-based work. Hence, the discussion on coaching practice for hybrid work is based on the available literature on selected areas of psychology of work and well-being. It is worth noting that hybrid work is a broad environmental condition influencing the health and well-being of individuals, hence, the application of coaching psychology to support individuals' development requires multiple approaches – for example, coaching for improving an individual's performance in the hybrid workplace, and coaching to support changes in individuals' working lifestyles.

A hybrid work approach can have both positive and negative implications. Table 9.1 provides a brief description of the advantages and disadvantages. The advantages are related to making remote work more purposeful using personal autonomy, flexibility and self-motivation to enable enhanced cognitive functions to accelerate performance, and to achieve a high level and quality of performance and production. The major disadvantages are minimal efforts to

Table 9.1 Hybrid work: implications for coaching practice

Advantages	Disadvantages
Personal autonomy	May not suit personal preference/personality type
Self-motivated	Loss of work identity
Flexibility	Work–family juggling
Personal space, creativity	Reduced collaborative learning
Less stress (travel, time)	Work environment inclusion issues
Economic	Technological affordance, availability
Enhanced cognitive functions	Communication problems
Family-friendly	Ineffective teamwork
Increased productivity	Lack of equality in task distribution

integrate in the work environment leading to less collaboration, communication barriers, invasion of work life into one's private life, equality issues in work distribution, and technological affordances and availability.

Individuals with an extrovert personality may resent hybrid work as it enforces isolation from their colleagues in a physical work environment, and it may bring identity loss as an employee where work identity is fitted around visible presence in a work environment or office (BBC Worklife 2021).

A coaching practitioner needs to consider how both hybrid work and office-based work affect an individual's performance, to address individuals' developmental and well-being issues. An attempt to search published evidence-based literature using databases on hybrid work coaching came up with no results. This was because the hybrid work style is not still widely accepted and endorsed by employer organizations, and as such, the need for coaching was not apparent in the transition to hybrid work at the present time. However, virtual or e-coaching, which forms a part of hybrid coaching, is increasingly being used by coaching psychology practitioners, and becoming an accepted standard for delivering to the remote work practice.

The following section presents a critical overview of virtual and e-coaching practice, highlighting the psychological principles regulating this area of practice. The main focus is to answer the key question of how coaching practice has developed and adapted in line with the changing demands of the environment in which individuals are continuously striving to achieve their full potential using a remote and virtual presence.

Virtual and e-coaching practice

A most recent advance in coaching practice is the delivery of virtual coaching, or e-coaching. This has been accelerated due to the pandemic and other environmental hazards. Virtual coaching has also been found to be effective in offering to the global community located in different remote areas. This has resulted in a growing body of evidence-based literature and increasing research. The voluminous literature on e-coaching is beyond the scope of this chapter, so I will only cover a few of the major critical issues contributing to knowledge and understanding of good practice in virtual coaching/e-coaching practice. This is nonetheless expected to generate research interests further, and spark debates on the comparative value of virtual and non-virtual coaching practices.

The definition of virtual coaching as a technology-aided coaching practice aiming to support development and growth is widely accepted. There are many varieties of virtual coaching practice due to the availability of advanced and rapidly changing technologies (Hultgren et al. 2016). For example, there is virtual coaching (coach and coachee interaction using virtual technologies), virtual self-coaching (self-administered computerized coaching programme/sessions), virtual reality coaching (predesigned use of an avatar for coaching on a virtual platform), AI coaching (software programmed to deliver coaching using a robot) and mixed virtual coaching (application of both physical and virtual coaching). Various technologies are used to deliver virtual/distance coaching, including telephone, virtual reality platforms, programmed sessions using avatars or robots, videos, audio and self-administered online sessions (Geissler et al. 2014). This implies that virtual/e-coaching, although a relatively recent development, is making fast progress with the invention of new technologies for education, health and social networking purposes. A brief discussion on the context of virtual/e-coaching is presented below to explain the viability and effectiveness of coaching practice using different virtual platforms.

Context of virtual/e-coaching

Virtual technologies were used in other disciplines such as counselling and psychotherapy during the 1970s. In the 1990s online learning began to have an important impact on the educational infrastructure of developed societies, and many educational institutions started endorsing online learning as an effective delivery technique. As such, a rapid increase in online learning was prevalent during the early twenty-first century. Online-only educational institutions were established at this time to attract a global learning community, remote learners and learners with special needs and learning difficulties. The ripple effect of online learning became apparent in all disciplines and it was widely recognized as an effective way to deliver learning. The influence of virtual reality, online platforms and e-technologies on coaching psychology practice is, however, a recent development, and this is because coaching psychology is a young discipline with a promising future.

There is growing evidence that virtual/e-coaching practice is effective, and various tools and models have been providing support for this (Eldridge and Dembkowski 2013). The impact of the Covid-19 pandemic on coaching practice opened up new modes of coaching delivery, such as online coaching and use of coaching bots and AI. These multiple delivery modes are strengthening the position of coaching psychology practice globally. A new way of working from home using online platforms has also impacted the coaching psychology profession. Many coaching practitioners have now adapted their practice to include virtual coaching. Hybrid working, alongside virtual coaching, is expected to dominate the practice both during and after the pandemic (Passmore et al. 2021).

It is important to understand the psychological constructs underpinning effective virtual/e-coaching. The following section provides a critical discussion about the influence of psychology knowledge on virtual/e-coaching practice to justify how virtual coaching practice is informed by psychological knowledge.

Virtual coaching psychology practice: critical issues

The fundamental principle on which coaching psychology practice is grounded refers to the facilitating process to support individuals to change, improve and reach their optimum level of performance. Virtual/e-coaching is delivered using this same key principle (individuals are capable of making change themselves) and the only difference is that it is delivered using an alternative delivery technique, technology-aided coaching. Unlike medicine and clinical psychology, coaching psychology is not governed by any prescriptive delivery technique, hence the effectiveness of technology-aided coaching practice cannot be undermined or undervalued.

The disadvantages due to the absence of human interaction in the coaching process are similar to other remote and e-learning activities. These are related to the impersonal nature of learning from the coaching intervention for both coachee and coaching practitioner, delivery techniques and 'fit for purpose' objectives, and issues of evaluating coaching outcomes. The compatibility of the coach–coachee interaction style in virtual coaching sessions is influenced by 'coach–coachee media fit' (Hultgren et al. 2016). This implies that both the coach and coachee must be advanced technology-literate to participate in e-coaching/virtual coaching sessions, and they must also have the same technological resources needed to follow the coaching intervention stages. This issue, however, restricts the user-friendliness and affordability of e-coaching practice. The application of this approach cannot be extended to those remote areas in the world where technology is still not widely used or available. This suggests that virtual coaching practice cannot overtake existing conventional coaching practice in terms of ease of administration, availability, affordability, costs and users' technological knowledge. The way forward then is the blended approach, like the blended learning practice offered in most educational institutions. The application of face-to-face coaching practice to complement virtual coaching practice is expected to continue to provide successful coaching outcomes, in which coachees' preferences, access needs and affordances are prioritized.

Virtual/e-coaching psychology is a recent practice-related development, so research has not yet reached the critical mass to validate the effectiveness of this type of coaching practice. There is also not yet extensive enough evaluation of this type of coaching practice to ascertain the advantages and disadvantages in comparison to face-to-face coaching practice (Burrous 2021). A few studies, however, have cautioned about the superficial advantages reported in virtual coaching sessions because of the nature of samples used and the coaching contexts. For example, coachees' virtual competency (Wang and Haggerty 2011) and experience of the virtual world can be advantages in delivering virtual coaching. However, developing mutual trust and understanding are present equally for both face-to-face and virtual coaching, although this can be difficult to establish in a virtual coaching session.

Due to the paucity of research evidence on the effectiveness of virtual/e-coaching intervention, the labelling of virtual work as second class (Caulat 2012), and the lack of theoretical models underpinning a virtual/e-coaching approach, it is difficult to be clear on coachees' knowledge and awareness of the value of virtual coaching, including the role of virtual coaching in providing enriched coaching experiences with skills enhancement for a coach. There is also controversy over the positive effects of using e-coaching exclusively, and preference is given to a blended approach (face-to-face and online). This is supporting the application of a blended coaching approach to address any disadvantages from virtual-only coaching intervention (Panteli and Chiasson 2008).

Drawing on the discussion above, Table 9.2 highlights the distinctive differences between face-to-face and virtual/e-coaching practice. Table 9.2 shows that the advantages and disadvantages of virtual and face-to-face coaching are distinctly different. For example, technology-supported virtual coaching offers personal autonomy, flexibility, a self-administered option to develop personal agency, authority and control over coachees' own behaviour to drive towards goal attainment. On the other hand, face-to-face coaching is usually a regulated and structured delivery in which flexibility and accessibility may not play a major part. A coachee may not have the option to reflect and self-appraise their performance during coaching sessions unless the delivery is designed to address this. However, face-to-face coaching delivers effective coaching outcomes through building trust and confidence, and clarity in task performance for a coachee. The blended approach can support developing personal agency, trust and confidence as well as provide instant feedback on coaching processes, including the opportunity for partnership with the coach to achieve the expected and effective coaching outcomes (LaBrosse 2007; Reyes 2009). There are a few shared advantages and disadvantages for face-to-face, virtual and blended coaching practice, and these are presented at the end of Table 9.2. They relate to issues of evaluation and effectiveness measures, research evidence to provide regulated knowledge, self-appraisal and developmental opportunity.

The following example showcases the effectiveness of blended coaching.

An example

An agricultural firm in a remote part of Northwest England had been failing to keep up their competitive advantage because of ongoing high absenteeism and

Table 9.2 Virtual vs face-to-face coaching practices: implications for coaching efficacy and effectiveness

	Technology-based	Face-to-face	Blended
Advantages	• Autonomy • Remote and global • Flexible • Accessible • Coachee-led/self-administered • Fast and self-paced	• Readiness to build trust • Mutual understanding • Reciprocal learning • Instant feedback and evaluation	• Increasing trust and confidence building • Task clarity, transparency • Personal autonomy • Immediate feedback, evaluation • Effective coaching outcome • Transferable skills
Disadvantages	• Impersonal • Trust and confidence issues • Complexity • Affordances • Accessibility • Lack of instant feedback and co-coaching	• Insensitive to remote delivery • Localized vs globalized issues • Lack of coachee autonomy • Less technology advance	• Complexity • Coachee preference • Accessibility • Affordability • Ease of administration • Compatibility
Shared advantages and disadvantages	Evaluation and effectiveness Research evidence Regulated knowledge delivery Self-appraisal and developmental	Evaluation and effectiveness Research evidence Regulated knowledge delivery Self-appraisal and developmental	Evaluation and effectiveness Research evidence Regulated knowledge delivery Self-appraisal and developmental

problems with recruiting competent and efficient employees. Despite business growth, employer–employee relations were causing serious concerns about production levels. With a high percentage of absenteeism, the business was almost on the verge of collapse. A coach was asked to support the business to recover from these difficult employee relations and to help the employees and employers to change and improve their behaviour.

The coach considered a blended coaching approach for two reasons. (a) Virtual/e-coaching would ensure natural response elicitation, as confidentiality of responses can be maintained and personal agency would improve, including confidence and partnership with the coaching process. It was used mainly for the purpose of exploring leadership style, employee satisfaction and perceived personal developmental needs and life goals. This can be the most effective practical approach for delivering coaching to a remote organization. (b) Face-to-face coaching was delivered to the management team using a team coaching approach, with a focus on supporting the management team to grow as a productive team, disregarding personal views and gains. Team coaching can help to optimize collective talent (Shams 2022). The development and change in performance from virtual coaching can then be enhanced in the face-to-face team coaching.

This hypothetical example shows that a blended coaching intervention is most effective when a coach needs to separate out complex issues affecting business growth from personal developmental issues. However, the coach needs to assess the nature of the coaching needs, situational factors, the context in which the intervention will be delivered, and the feasibility of a blended coaching approach. In addition, advanced technology literacy and familiarity with technology-friendly coaching intervention strategies must accompany the coaching competency requirement. The factors outlined under disadvantages in Table 9.2 also apply to a coach.

The limited research evidence on virtual/e-coaching and blended coaching has made it difficult to provide a critical insight into the effectiveness of this approach in coaching delivery. However, the underlying psychological principle of behavioural change through feedback and facilitation in an e-coaching intervention is evident.

There is increasing interest in artificial intelligence coaching (AI coaching) due to the popular use of artificial intelligence in business and educational enquiries (Lai 2017). However, AI is still not accounted as a viable option for effective coaching intervention (Passmore et al. 2021). The main reason is that the powerful influence of human presence in coaching cannot be denied. Face-to-face coaching practice has a very important role in generating developmental interests for a coachee aiming to excel in performance to attain their goals.

One of the distinctive features of coaching psychology practice is the wide application irrespective of the socio-demographic characteristics of coachees. Although the techniques and tools, approaches and method of delivery may vary according to which non-clinical population groups are seeking coaching psychology interventions, the fundamental principle of coaching psychology practice remains the same for all. This relates to change, development, enhancement and progress. The universal appeal needs to be discussed in a global and local coaching context to augment our understanding of the immense value of coaching psychology practice across all cultures and societies.

A critical overview of the existing literature and key issues influencing global and localized coaching practice is presented in the next section.

An overview of coaching psychology practice: global and local contexts

Coaching psychology is localized, Eurocentric and Westernized. The reason behind this is that it is a new discipline, mainly emerging in the early twentieth century and gaining popular momentum during the early twenty-first century in the Western context. Coaching psychology practice and coaching research have been localized since the inception of this discipline. Interest in developing coaching psychology practice in Asia and Africa has been generated quite recently, however, there is not enough research-based evidence or theoretical models of coaching practices in these cultural contexts.

Coaching practice applied in different countries can help to advance coaching psychology globally (Gentry et al. 2013), and cultural context is an important factor in understanding the application of coaching psychology practice across all cultures (Rousseau and Fried 2001). There is still not enough research on distinctive approaches and techniques used to coach different cultural groups. A few studies, however, have indicated the differences in perceived best practice in coaching. For example, Gentry and colleagues (2013) conducted a qualitative comparative study using coaches from Asia and Europe. They found that achieving effective coaching outcomes was identified as the best practice in coaching by Asian coaches, whereas coaches from Europe believed professional competency of coaches can ensure best coaching practice. However, similarities in valuing relationship building with a strong coachee-focused approach, coaching tool selection and cultural awareness were also found.

Coaching psychology practice is not about applying a 'one-size-fits-all' model (Abbott 2010). Hence, contextual differences and diversity in cultural practices must be taken into consideration to conceive coachees' expected change in behaviour as determined by the cultural context (Lowman 2007; Peterson 2007). The significant differences in the application of the same coaching intervention programme, even within Europe indicates the subtle cultural differences between all cultures, irrespective of their close proximity geographically (van Hoye et al. 2015). Although the cross-cultural transferability of the coaching programme can be attested, however, coaching implementation processes are varied according to the culturally driven needs of the specific individuals and organizations.

Human behaviour is contextualized, and is the by-product of cultural practice, as such, the process through which individuals strive to achieve optimum performance level will differ across various cultures (Shams 2002, 2005). The perceived best coaching practice can influence the coaching intervention stages and subsequently the coaching outcomes.

More research and professional initiatives can help to popularize coaching psychology practice in various countries around the world. One such initiative is the launch of the *Journal of Coaching, Consulting and Coaching Psychology in Africa* by the Africa Board for Coaching, Consulting and Coaching Psychology in 2014, which aims to develop and promote coaching practices in an African context, and present contesting ideas and views to justify the development of coaching practice for Africa by Africa. Similar ventures across Asia, the Far East and other parts of the world not only can help coaching psychology practices to flourish, but can also enrich coaching psychology knowledge and enhance good, effective practices in coaching as a context-free intervention for supporting individuals' development and growth.

A database search for coaching psychology in Asia yielded only a few results. They indicate the predominant application of a solution-focused coaching approach in Asia (Szabo and Hogan 2017). However, this is mainly prevalent in a few selected countries in Asia. Coaching psychology as a discipline and coaching practice underpinned by psychological knowledge are still not yet fully developed and recognized in many countries either within or beyond Asia.

Figures 9.1, 9.2 and 9.3 represent the distinctive features of local and global coaching interventions.

Figure 9.1 Upward mobility of local coaching practice

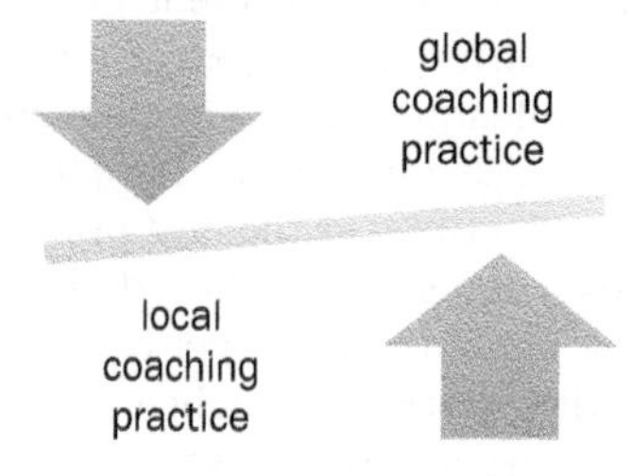

Figure 9.2 Distinctive features of local coaching practice

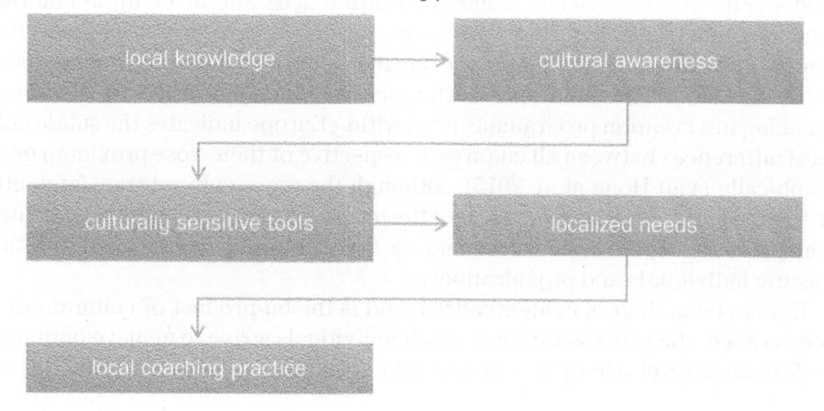

Figure 9.3 Key elements in global coaching practice

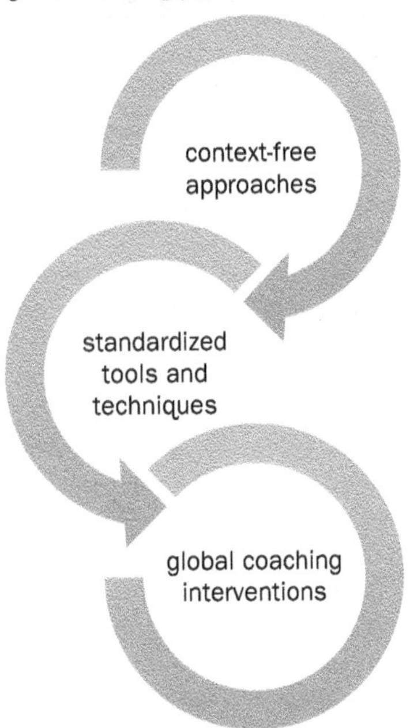

Figure 9.1 displays the upward mobility of local coaching practice. For example, culturally sensitive coaching tools and techniques can be applied at the global level to serve the heterogeneous population groups. Local coaching practice is grounded on local knowledge, and local needs are served using culturally sensitive tools (Figure 9.2). A global coaching approach can be effective, with standardized tools and context-free approaches. A context-free approach is characterized by awareness of diversity in behavioural performance across different cultures. Differences in coaching practice within a region mean there is a need to explore the issues affecting coaching intervention in a local context. For example, van Hoye et al. (2015) have found differences between France and Norway in the implementation processes of empowering coaching training programmes for trained coaching educators, implying that apparent cultural similarities within a single geographical region cannot guarantee uniformity in coaching practice. However, the research did not provide detailed information of the application of a psychological model and tools in the implementation process, and as such the research mainly addresses coaching practice in general.

I hope the discussion in this section will generate interest among aspiring coaching practitioners to contribute both at a local and global level. Coaching psychology thus has huge potential to support individuals' growth and development in a local and global context.

The contribution of coaching psychology to society

The contribution of coaching psychology to all areas in society is increasingly evident, from formal endorsement of coaching psychology practice to increased interest in developing courses and programmes in the education sector, sports and personal development, and leadership development in the health and business sectors. The main attraction of coaching psychology is the emphasis on supporting the development of non-clinical population groups. This drives many sectors in society to call for coaching psychology interventions for their respective areas. Coaching psychology thus has a wide scope and impact on the efficient functioning of society in general, and specific effects on individuals' performance levels and enhancement in almost all sectors of society.

The contribution of coaching psychology to four major areas of society – education, business, health and sports – is presented in Figure 9.4. The specific areas from each of these four major sectors are the prime focus of a coaching intervention for behavioural change and performance enhancement. Coaching intervention in the education sector is to support students' learning and development to attain expected learning goals using relevant coaching approaches, tools and techniques. Similarly, business coaching focuses on leadership development, accelerating team performance and improving interpersonal relations. Business coaching is also delivered to sports sectors to support sports organizations to enhance their business functions, paying attention to individuals' personal and professional development. Health and sports coaching is delivered to support health behaviour changes and well-being improvement, including individuals' performance enhancement at both personal and professional levels.

Coaching psychology provides the platform for an individual to unfold their full potential, and to achieve sustainable progressive changes in behaviour to attain their desired life goals. Hence, coaching psychology practice can help society to recover from skill shortages, and deliver improvements in health and

Figure 9.4 Contribution of coaching psychology to major areas of society

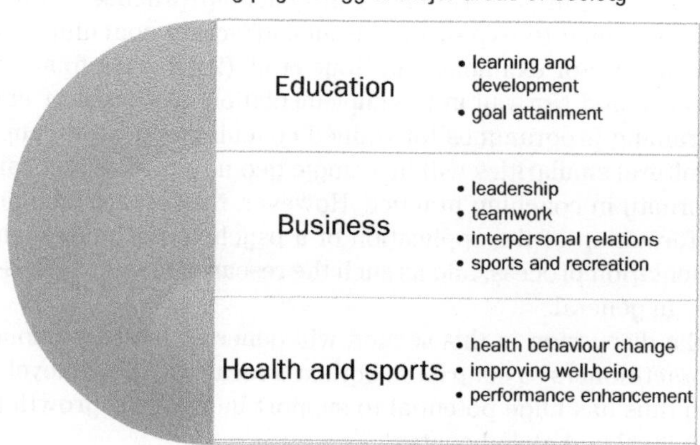

well-being using individuals themselves as the main drivers of all changes. The only critical issue affecting coaching psychology is the formalization and validation of the practice to safeguard the public from any shortfalls in practices and interventions.

Conclusion

Coaching psychology is developing fast, implying the powerful influence of coaching psychology practice on individuals' development, which is subject to continuous changes in line with changing environmental demands. The discussion in this chapter has highlighted the most recent changes in coaching practice, and how coaching psychology practice is evolving due to changing environmental challenges. The discussions on coaching for hybrid work and virtual working confirm the agile scientific status of coaching psychology practice, which will place coaching psychology at the forefront of all psychological practices to benefit individuals and societies at both a local and global level.

More evidence-based research and increasing innovative practices, along with developing knowledge depth in coaching psychology, can ensure the effective delivery of coaching psychology for the new generation. Coaching psychology practice can reach implementation science status if continuous implementation of coaching practice evaluation is undertaken to find out if the coaching outcomes are influenced by the theoretical model applied or the intervention processes (van Hoye et al. 2015). This is important for coaching psychology as it is mainly a practice-based discipline, and a rigorous evaluation of the implementation of coaching outcomes can validate the practice, and help to gain recognition as a reliable scientific practice to develop individuals to their optimum level. Implementation science offers five stages of effective implementation – reach, effectiveness, adoption, implementation and maintenance (Glasgow et al. 2006). Reach refers to targeting individuals seeking coaching; effectiveness is the impact of the coaching outcome on individuals' behaviour; adoption is the wide acceptance of coaching intervention programmes; the efficacy of application is implementation; and maintenance is the sustainability of the changes caused by coaching outcomes.

Coaching psychology is very close to achieving all these stages, and a discipline-based initiative and professional movement are needed to complete each stage to reach the goal of a fully grown, applied scientific discipline.

References

Abbott, G.N. (2010) Cross-cultural coaching: A paradoxical perspective, in E. Cox, T. Bachkirova and D. Clutterbuck (eds) *The Complete Handbook of Coaching*. Oxford: Blackwell Publishing, pp. 324–40.

BBC worklife (2021) What is BBC Worklife?, BBC website. Available at: https://www.bbc.com/worklife/article/20190721-what-is-bbc-worklife (accessed 21 September 2021).

Burrous, T.C. (2021) A comparison study on e-coaching and face-to-face coaching, *Dissertation Abstracts International Section B: The Sciences and Engineering*, 82(12-B).

Caulat, G. (2012) *Virtual Leadership*. Faringdon: Libri Publishing.

Eldridge, F. and Dembkowski, S. (2013) Behavioral coaching, in J. Passmore, D.B. Peterson and T. Freire (eds) *The Wiley-Blackwell Handbook of the Psychology of Coaching and Mentoring*. Oxford: Wiley-Blackwell, pp. 298–318.

Geissler, H., Hasenbein, M., Kanatouri, S. and Wegener, R. (2014) E-coaching: Conceptual and empirical findings of a virtual coaching programme, *International Journal of Evidence Based Coaching and Mentoring*, 12(2): 165–87.

Gentry, W.A., Manning, L., Wolf, A.K., Hernez-Broome, G., Allen, L.W. (2013) What coaches believe are best practices for coaching: A qualitative study of interviews from coaches residing in Asia and Europe, *Journal of Leadership Studies*, 7(2): 18–31.

Glasgow, R.E., Klesges, L.M., Dzewaltowski, D.A., Estabrooks, P.A. and Vogt, T.M. (2006) Evaluating the impact of health promotion programs: Using the RE-AIM framework to form summary measures for decision making involving complex issues, *Health Education Research*, 21(5): 688–94.

Hultgren, U., Palmer, S. and O'Riordan, S. (2016) Developing and evaluating a virtual coaching programme: A pilot study, *The Coaching Psychologist*, 12(2): 67–75.

LaBrosse, M. (2007) Working successfully in a virtual world, *Employment Relations Today*, 34(3): 85–90.

Lai, P.C. (2017) The literature review of technology adoption models and theories for the novelty technology, *Journal of Information Systems and Technology Management*, 14(1): 21–38.

Lowman, R.L. (2007) Coaching and consulting in multicultural contexts: Integrating themes and issues, *Consulting Psychology Journal: Practice and Research*, 59(4): 296–303.

Panteli, N. and Chiasson, M. (2008) *Exploring Virtuality Within and Beyond Organizations*. Basingstoke: Palgrave Macmillan.

Passmore, J., Liu, Q. and Tewald, S. (2021) Future trends in coaching: Results from a global coach survey, 2021, *The Coaching Psychologist*, 17(2): 41–52.

Peterson, D. (2007) Executive coaching in a cross-cultural context, *Consulting Psychology Journal: Practice and Research*, 59(4): 261–70.

Reyes, A. (2009) Coaching virtual global leaders: The communications challenge, *International Journal of Coaching in Organizations*, 7(2): 122–36.

Rousseau, D.M. and Fried, Y. (2001) Location, location, location: Contextualizing organizational research, *Journal of Organizational Behavior*, 22(1): 1–13.

Shams, M. (2002) Issues in the study of indigenous psychologies: Historical perspectives, cultural interdependence and institutional regulations, *Asian Journal of Social Psychology*, 5(2): 79–91.

Shams, M. (2005) Developmental issues in indigenous psychology: Sustainability and local knowledge, *Asian Journal of Social Psychology*, 8(1): 39–50.

Shams, M. (2022) Team coaching in family business, in M. Shams (2022), *Supporting the Family Business: A Coaching Practitioner's Handbook*, 2nd edn. New York: Routledge, pp. 150–60.

Szabo, P. and Hogan, D. (2017) Introduction to solution focused practice in coaching in Asia, in D. Hogan, D. Hogan, J. Tuomola and A.K.L. Yeo (eds) *Solution Focused Practice in Asia*. New York: Routledge, pp. 185–90.

van Hoye, A., Larsen, T., Sovik, M. et al. (2015) Evaluation of the Coaches Educators training implementation of the PAPA project: A comparison between Norway and France, *Scandinavian Journal of Medicine & Science in Sports*, 25(5): e539–e546.

Wang, Y. and Haggerty, N. (2011) Individual virtual competence and its influence on work outcomes, *Journal of Management Information Systems*, 27(4): 299–334.

10 Emerging issues in coaching psychology practice

Manfusa Shams

Summary

The knowledge gained from coaching psychology practice and evidence-based research is illuminating our understanding of holistic development, and the role of individuals as active agents to change, improve and progress on their desired goals using their own personal resources, which is embodied in neurological and cognitive functions and manifested in behavioural responses. This book has presented the immense value of the theoretical basis of coaching psychology practice, and offered a new paradigm of coaching psychology practice using the selective realism conceptual model. This chapter draws conclusions, based on all the chapters, to present the emerging issues in coaching psychology practice and a set of key areas for further development. This discussion is needed for appropriate theorizing of coaching psychology to apply to practice, and to meet the demand for the recognition of coaching psychology as a valuable applied scientific discipline from the educational and service providers' perspectives, and at a regulated national and international level.

Keywords: psychology in coaching, epistemology and ontology, situational realism, coaching psychology, performance science, selective realism.

Introduction

Coaching psychology is a relatively new discipline although the concept of 'coaching' has been used in the sports and art industries for many years. It involves the application of relevant psychological principles, theories and concepts, hence it is essential to develop a psychology discipline-based approach in coaching practice. Coaching psychology practice, as a disciplinary approach to map the psychological growth and effective functioning of individuals as a result of coaching, was established with the first formal recognition of the Special Group in Coaching Psychology from the Australian Psychological Society in 2002, followed by the British Psychological Society in 2004

(Whybrow and Palmer 2006). Since then, coaching psychology has developed fast worldwide, e.g. in Denmark, New Zealand, South Africa and Sweden. The institutional support and endorsements of professional psychological societies were instrumental in increasing the attention of academics, practitioners, policymakers, businesses, etc. to developing and popularizing coaching psychology, and to appreciating, valuing and acknowledging the positive influence of coaching intervention for making sustainable changes in individuals' functioning systems.

The need to theorize coaching psychology and conceptual development to advance the discipline and professional practice is growing with the demands for coaching psychology practice. The discussions in all chapters have reaffirmed the value of coaching psychology as a professional practice to support human functioning to an optimum level.

Coaching psychology practice helps to foster growth in psychological functioning, optimizing human potential, enhancing performance, development and well-being in wide population groups. The distinctive feature of this discipline is the important contribution to different specialist areas (e.g. education, business, occupations, health and well-being), with a focus on application and practice (intervention and change). Coaching psychology is delivering psychological knowledge using coaching as a vehicle to understand human development. The main focus is on the optimization of human potential for further growth and development.

Coaching psychology is an applied discipline, and is developing fast due to increasing demand from users and services in all sectors. Unlike any other psychology sub-discipline, coaching psychology is evolving on 'application and practice'. Hence, coaching practitioners and coaching psychologists are playing a significant role to plan, develop and deliver coaching interventions using relevant psychological knowledge and research evidence. It is important to focus on the practitioner's perspective to deliver effective coaching intervention, as coaching psychology is predominantly a practice-focused psychology discipline. A systematic approach to delivering knowledge about the practical application of coaching psychology to different areas of human behaviour, and to developing appropriate professional skills to improve coaching practice is required to justify the prominent role of coaching psychology in practice.

The strong presence of psychology in coaching practice is the main feature of this discipline, hence a discussion on the influence of psychological principles and knowledge in coaching delivery is needed. This book has served this need using relevant evidence-based discussion, practitioners' critical reflective accounts, theoretical formulations and conceptual development, paying attention to the coach and coachee as the two primary active agents in the coaching intervention process.

Part I (practice) offered a theory-focused approach. The chapters in this section contain critical discussions and analyses of the development of coaching psychology practice from the perspective of a few selected schools of thought (Chapter 2). The persuasive argument in favour of the influence of psychological principles, concepts and constructs on developing theories and theoretical models of coaching psychology practice is discussed in Chapter 1. A new conceptual model supporting the development of a new coaching psychology knowledge paradigm was the main attraction in this part (Chapter 4), including the essential ethical and professional issues underlying good practice in coaching psychology (Chapter 3).

In Part II, theoretical knowledge derived from selected schools of thought is translated into practical application (Chapter 5), including conceptual development for practice (Chapter 6), characteristics of a coachee to achieve effective coaching outcomes (Chapter 8), major developmental issues in coaching psychology practice (Chapter 7), and new ways of delivering coaching practice (Chapter 9). The main theme running through all the chapters is 'psychology in coaching practice'. Existing coaching psychology practice is predominantly localized, and a call for a global initiative to popularize and implement coaching practice across all societies is discussed in Chapter 9. The discussion in all chapters has used relevant theoretical models, schools of thought and evidence-based analyses to justify the distinctive features of coaching psychology as a scientific, practice-based applied science. The practical application of coaching psychology is grounded on a relevant conceptual framework and theoretical base. All the chapters in Part II highlighted the value of theoretical underpinning for effective coaching practice.

A summary of the major emerging critical issues from the discussions in all chapters is presented below.

Emerging issues

Psychology in coaching

Coaching psychology practice is characterized by the application of psychology knowledge and principles in a coaching context. It is a scientific discipline with special features of psychological knowledge, and applied to achieve behavioural optimization and goal attainment. The discussion in Chapter 1 highlights that the major features of general psychology are embedded in coaching psychology practice, hence coaching psychology is a branch of its parent psychology discipline. Coaching practice using psychological knowledge in relevant areas to support individuals' self-growth and incremental progression in goal attainment is increasingly valued and recognized by other areas of psychology, users of coaching psychology practice and policymakers in major social systems such as health care and education.

Coaching psychology is focused on supporting individuals' development, with an emphasis on personal agency to change and improve. The essential knowledge coaching psychology offers is predominantly grounded on humanistic and positive psychology, although various other psychological schools of thought are increasingly influencing coaching practice, for example, gestalt and existential psychology (Chapter 5).

Coaching psychology, epistemology and ontology

Coaching psychology knowledge is not generated naturally, and the question is how knowledge of coaching psychology is constructed. What is coaching psychology knowledge and how has this knowledge evolved from coaching practice?

Psychological knowledge is constructed from debating different schools of thought, as one ideology was rejected to support another emerging ideology. For example, structuralism was rejected by behaviourism. From this perspective, coaching psychology did not originate from any specific school of thought; rather it is emerging as a unique discipline using multiple bases of psychological knowledge to change and improve behaviour. Evidence-based behavioural change in reaction to coaching practice has generated knowledge about innate human potential. This knowledge was valued and applied in the practice without subsuming the knowledge under a theory of knowing. If people are able to develop to their full potential with the help of the environmental stimuli, then the natural sequence of environmental influence can provide further insights into the nature and extent of influences for making behavioural changes. Coaching intervention may form a part of environmental influence, and the knowledge gained from the intervention may extend our understanding of the way self-knowledge is evolved and transformed. The continuous negotiation using one's own thinking and problem-solving approach may help individuals to reinvent themselves in the light of new thinking, exploring creative solutions towards progression and attainment. The chain of inner thoughts during the coaching intervention may assist the coachee's capabilities to direct their own behavioural responses towards self-growth and developmental progression.

Coaching psychology is an excellent subject for understanding the way knowledge is created during coaching intervention, and how this new knowledge is transformed into self-help actions, providing depth in learning about one's self. Understanding one's own self is supported and reinforced in coaching psychology practice, and as such, knowledge generated from coaching psychology practice is authentic and reliable.

Situational realism in coaching practice

A coaching intervention is an effective mechanism to help an individual to explore their real self in relation to the environmental demands, using their neurological, cognitive and affective receptors. Petocz and Mackay (2013) define situational realism as the study of those organism–environment relations and interactions (dynamic systems) that involve cognition, motivation and emotion. The idea of situational realism originates from pre-Socratic (Heraclitean) and Aristotelian philosophical thought. It provides a new paradigm in understanding behavioural change in terms of understanding reality through experience (Groarke 2009).

The selective realism model presented in Chapter 4 is built on the concept of situational realism to affirm that coachee–coaching environmental relations and interactions bring changes in biological systems (brain functions), and stimulate sensory functions to improve cognition and behavioural performance.

Realism is not limited to being aware of the environment, but refers to complex information processing involving neurological, cognitive and behavioural functions about how the environment is perceived, responded to and stored for the desired changes and improvement (Tonneau 2004). The discussion on situational realism furthermore asserts that realism allows people to develop agency over the present moment in the environment (Chirkov 2021). A coaching intervention can empower an individual to achieve the personal agency to self-reflect, and interpret the meanings of the present experience to further develop cognitive and behavioural functions. An individual thus relives their own life experiences in the light of changes through the coaching sessions, which is expected to influence and transform their present thinking, feelings and actions upward for further optimization. The selective realism conceptual model proposed in Chapter 4 highlights these selective live experiences from coaching interventions, and the significant impact on an individual's total functioning systems (neurological, cognitive and behavioural) for further development and optimization.

Coaching psychology is a performance science

Coaching psychology is a special vehicle on the road of performance. An effective coaching practice accelerates performance towards goal attainment. Hence, this discipline is a behavioural science with specialist attention to performance. The discussions in all chapters are focused on behavioural issues, and the powerful influence of a coaching intervention to help a coachee to excel in behavioural performance. However, behavioural performance does not function in isolation, and is accompanied by cognitive and neurological functional changes. Coaching psychology practice thus delivers an inclusive performance change and improvement for an individual. The active role of a coachee during coaching sessions supports their powerful personal agency to influence the coaching outcome (Chapter 8).

Usually sports and exercise science, and sports coaching are regarded as performance sciences as these disciplines study overt changes in behavioural performance which can be measured and replicated. However, I am arguing in favour of all types of performances as a result of coaching intervention. These include neurological, cognitive and behavioural performances. The proposed selective realism conceptual model has included these multiple elements in individuals' performance. Although coaching psychology practice is explicitly directed towards supporting individuals to engage in a self-help approach to achieve their desired behavioural outcomes, this practice is also recognized as a strong guide for accelerating performance to the maximum level (Jones et al. 2016).

In coaching psychology, a coachee has the autonomy to steer through their performance to reach the goal – coaching practice does not follow the 'one-size-fits-all' approach to coaching sessions (Salas and Kozlowski 2010). Coaching psychology practice considers a goal-setting approach in which a set of activities and performance-related assessments are delivered to support a coachee in understanding, and reflecting on their present behaviour to remove the barriers to achieving behavioural progression in the designated area. Good coaching practice supports developing realization, awareness and developmental understanding using personalized and experiential learning, and reflective understanding of 'self'. The learning from the coaching sessions becomes declarative and provides new procedural knowledge which can be applied to improve understanding of self, and this can eventually lead to a number of behavioural performances, such as self-efficacy and confidence, increased satisfaction, awareness and motivation (Jones et al. 2016). Performance is not limited to behavioural outcomes, but also improvement in cognitive and affective outcomes (Kraiger et al. 1993).

There is a need for more theoretical and conceptual development of coaching psychology as a practice-based scientific discipline. This can provide new direction for understanding the influence of psychology in coaching practice, with affirmation that coaching psychology is a behavioural and performance science, and the practice of coaching psychology helps to change and improve neurological, cognitive and behavioural performances.

Key areas for further development

Coaching psychology is an emerging scientific discipline. Hence, further progress is required in theorizing, conceptual development and evidence-based coaching practice. Development in these areas can ensure the smooth progression of this new discipline, and provide depth in our understanding of human behaviour using a coaching psychology lens.

Professional development of coaching practitioners and ethical issues in coaching practice are two important areas for further development. A rigorous training and formal accreditation procedure can pave the way for coaching psychology to establish itself as a regulated and accredited practice-based scientific discipline. The dominant influence of localized coaching practice on existing practice, and the need for a globalized coaching psychology practice require further research and collaboration from across different societies. The advancement of coaching psychology in parallel with major environmental changes must be ensured to serve the changing needs of individuals, and this area needs further development. The interdisciplinary approach in coaching psychology practice is not yet fully explored and requires evidence-based research to put into practice.

The educational value inherent in coaching psychology, and the scope to formalize coaching psychology programmes in higher education to achieve a professional qualification have still not been fully explored and recognized. This area needs immediate attention from policymakers and education providers to offer coaching psychology as an important human science.

Conclusion

The major feature of this book is the discussion on the theoretical basis of coaching psychology, conceptual development of coaching psychology practice, the value of ethically driven coaching practice, interdisciplinary and diverse coaching practice in the context of new ways of working, and a focused approach on the coachee as the determinant of effective coaching outcomes. Each chapter has provided evidence-based discussion on the influence of psychological knowledge, concepts and theories on coaching practice, with an affirmation that coaching practice is grounded on psychological principles and theoretical constructs including several major schools of thought.

Coaching psychology has entered the limelight of professional practice, with increasing interest in, and attention to, developing and endorsing this new emerging discipline as a valuable part of behavioural science. This is encouraging for coaching psychology practitioners to develop their professional careers, and to support the growth of this practice to benefit the wider society.

Coaching psychology is on the edge of achieving a competitive advantage as it serves all areas of human functions without any clinical diagnostic procedures, clinical trials or assessments. Coaching practice has the potential to empower individuals to increase their self-knowledge and understanding, and develop themselves fully in relation to the environmental demands and available resources. Coaching psychology is emerging as a popular and valuable scientific discipline with applications to each area of human life. This discipline will be an essential knowledge base for understanding human behaviour, and for advancing our comprehension of complexities around human behaviour in relation to the changing and unpredictable environment in which we live.

In this book all the leading coaching psychologists and practitioner authors have presented their persuasive arguments for asserting the importance of psychologizing coaching practice, and the value of delivering coaching practice underpinned by solid and appropriate theories, ethical framework and conceptual models. The theoretical basis of coaching practice is presented eloquently in this book: this distinctive feature is expected to serve as an essential companion of coaching practice, a guide for practitioners, and a landmark in the theory of the coaching psychology discipline.

References

Chirkov, V. (2021) Reflections on an application of realism in psychology, *Theory & Psychology*, 31(3): 455–9.

Groarke, L. (2009) *An Aristotelian Account of Induction*. Montreal: McGill-Queen's University Press.

Jones, R.J., Woods, S.A. and Guillaume, Y.R.F. (2016) The effectiveness of workplace coaching: A meta-analysis of learning and performance outcomes from coaching, *Journal of Occupational and Organizational Psychology*, 89(2): 249–77.

Kraiger, K., Ford, J.K. and Salas, E.D. (1993) Application of cognitive, skill-based, and affective theories of learning outcomes to new methods of training evaluation, *Journal of Applied Psychology*, 78(2): 311–28.

Petocz, A. and Mackay, N. (2013) Unifying psychology through situational realism, *Review of General Psychology*, 17(2): 216–23.

Salas, E. and Kozlowski, S.W.J. (2010) Learning, training, and development in organizations: Much progress and a peek over the horizon, in S.W.J. Kozlowski and E. Salas (eds) *Learning, Training, and Development in Organizations*. New York: Routledge, pp. 3–64.

Tonneau, F. (2004) Consciousness outside the head, *Behaviour and Philosophy*, 32(1): 97–123.

Whybrow, A. and Palmer, S. (2006) The coaching psychology movement and its development within the British Psychological Society, *International Coaching Psychology Review*, 1(1): 5–11.

Index

Page numbers in italics are figures.